How Following the Masses Takes You Away from Success

THE CONVINCING LIE

SHIVRATAN MAHESHKANT MISHRA

This is a work of nonfiction. The events and the incidents mentioned in the book are true and real. However, some names and characteristics have been changed, some events have been compressed, and some dialogues have been recreated

First Edition: June 2025
Printed in India

Printed at Trinity Academy, Mumbai
Typeset in EB Garamond
ISBN: 978-93-6070-238-0

Cover Design: Prajakta Sawant

STORYMIRROR
Stories that reflect you

Publisher:	StoryMirror Infotech Pvt. Ltd. Unit No-F/705, 7th Floor Kailas Corporate Lounge, Veer Savarkar Road, Vikhroli Park Site, Vikhroli West, Mumbai-400079, Maharashtra, India.
Web:	storymirror.com
Facebook:	@storymirror
Instagram:	@storymirror
Twitter:	@story_mirror
Contact Us:	marketing@storymirror.com

ACKNOWLEDGEMENTS

The truest way to honour your mentors is to embody the wisdom they instilled in you. I wish to start the book by thanking all those leaders who shaped the version of me that speaks through pages of this book. You shaped my value system, my approach, helped me build my base and set direction to a curious follower.

Maheshkant Mishra

Aruna Mishra

Santoshi Mishra

Vasudev Nayak

Mr. Shyam Patil

Dr. Ratnadip Joshi

Dr. J. P. George

Dr. Dipti Sakhre

Anil Bhat

Dr. Mahesh Goudar

Sai Sridhar

Vinayaka Nagaraja

Raghav Gulur

Keni Satish

Deepak Vaidyanathan

Shankar Chandrasekar

Parthiv Shah

Srinivas Nanjappa

You instituted, restructured and changed few blocks of my core, you looked through my intent and trusted in me, gave me a pathway to evolve a bit every day.

Thanks to all my mentees, those who gave me confidence and believed in my value system, thanks for living this journey of evolving together and learning mutually. I value you, you are extremely important to me, let us continue to talk until we become a version of each other.

Thank you, my cohorts, from IIMC, SMP 19, Parul Kamra, Payal Nambiar, Vikrant Sood, Vivek Kaushal, Harsh Varma, Vishal and Anand, you all directly indirectly contributed to the finalization of this book.

Special thanks to Adil Baig, for giving the most relevant title to the book, a journey we lived together.

Thanks to Tejaswi Yavatakar for her constant support as a friend and family.

Brain is designed to take the adversity both ways, as a lesson or as a failure. More often than not, its how we choose to see it that makes all the difference.

INTRODUCTION

I wonder if the sequence of things happening in a day, in a year and around the decade of your life matters.

The below anecdote may not make any sense in the era of digitalization and Google Maps. However, back in 1998, finding an address was less easy.

In 1998, I was in class 4 when my father was operated on for a herniated disc in the Apex Hospital, Borivali. My mother didn't sleep at all the night before the surgery, nor during the day while the surgery was underway. These were the days when Physiotherapy barely existed in India and its significance was not known. A herniated disc could cause months of no work, no job and no movements for a middle-aged individual like my father. My father struggled for an entire 8-month period during which my mother was the captain of our house. The anecdote is less about my father's surgery and more about a silly accidental detour that I ended up in.

I was too young to comprehend the weight of my mother's pain when the surgery began. Yet, however, I found myself crying alongside her – not out of understanding but simply because she was crying. Clinging to her outside the hospital doors, we held each other in silence, counting the endless hours. She had to take care of my father, his hospital visits, the finances of the house, raising three children, and many other factors – almost causing mental breakdown – yet she was strong enough to deal with it.

As soon as the surgery was over, I asked my mother if she could buy me something to eat. We both were food deprived; however, I alone felt the hunger. Eight long hours after my father's exit from the Operation Theater (OT), he finally regained consciousness. I couldn't suppress my hunger anymore and ended up asking, "Mummy, can we get something to eat?" She happily took me out. We crossed the road and walked 30 meters ahead to identify a Pan shop, where we got biscuits too. My mother bought me Parle G. I was happy and we started walking back to the hospital. Suddenly, my mother sensed that she had lost her way. She almost panicked. "I can't see the hospital road... where is the gully?" I told her that it was right in front of the Pan shop and we may be a little walk further. I have an Eidetic memory, the hospital and the route to the Pan shop were printed in my head, yet my mother could barely figure out. We kept walking on the other side of the hospital, going meters away instead of getting closer. She kept asking the people around about the hospital address, yet no one seemed to be aware. The struggle continued and we walked almost more than 1 km away from the venue and it kept getting darker. By now mother started crying.

I now understand what she was going through. She had been fighting a battle for 8 months and right when it seemed to hit a milestone where things would start unfolding for the better, she left one loose end and it felt like losing another unanticipated battle. This is the era where movies were based on siblings losing their families in Kumbh ka Mela, accidental separation due to misleading route was a thing, especially when my mother had lost her own mother in a similar situation. My grandmother could never be traced again after she boarded a wrong bus.

My mother was scolding me, venting out as she felt that no road could lead us to the destination. I began crying too, I said I'm sorry, I won't eat biscuit ever again. We kept walking and despite crying, I read a note on the wall written in red, that said,

"Ali angawar, ghetli shingawar!"

In Marathi, it translates to,

"I faced my challenges head-on, embraced it, and wore it as a crown!"

It took me a few minutes to decipher the meaning. The image of a man with horns helped – signifying defiance & strength. Somehow, it helped me identify the chaos as an opportunity. Not sure what changed, I was barely 9 years old. I firmly asked my mother to take me to the Pan shop again – the one we visited first. She didn't take my request until I once again assured her, 'Mother, take me to the Pan shop, from there we can find the hospital!'

We were more than a kilometer away, yet it was easy for her to walk back the trained path. Once we were at the shop, I directed her to cross the road and walk the opposite way, there was a gully and there we were! Mummy saw the hospital board and took a sigh of relief. To this day, I have no idea how it happened. However, it was the first time ever in my life that I took control of a situation. Being a slow-witted kid in an extremely high IQ family, the moment was surreal - unimaginable. It was the first moment when I solved a problem unintentionally created by me.

Finally, we met Papa and shared the story, it took me many years to overcome the fear. For nearly 4-6 years after, I would think of that detour and get anxious, yet I would tell myself to never repeat the mistake and ensure to remember the route well.

Even today, I assure my brain that the detour was an organized trouble caused by the universe for me, it was purely for me to read the script on the wall, it was an idiom that designed my brain to function the way I do until date. I wish to tell my mother one day - that detour was the biggest success hack I learnt!

The story is not about my father or mother, it is more about the wall and the words etched into it. Every time I end up in trouble or lost in disguise, I try to find the wall with a script. There would not always be a physical wall, however, there would always be a takeaway script, no matter how big or unsolvable the problem is!

I still do not know if universe constructs a problem for us to specifically learn. But I do know that most certainly our *brain is designed to take adversity both ways, as a lesson or as a failure. More often than not, it's how we choose to see it that makes all the difference.*

If this book can have a few takeaways, the most essential that my readers must resonate shall be,

"Jar ali angawar, tar mee ghenar shingawar!"

(If it comes my way, I'll embrace it as my crown.)

A sketchy exercise:

Consider you are in a conference room; you end up listening to Simon Sinek's first live interview. The dais is open to Q and A and the microphone is rolled over to the audience.

Hypothetically, by the end of reading this line, you must raise your hand imitating that you have a question to ask (please raise, don't lose this, do it). Even if you are at the airport, in a crowd full of people or in your bedroom or dining alone, you must mock this test physically.

If you didn't even try raising your hand, you felt it wasn't necessary, my friend, you are too sensitive or you aren't ready to read the book yet.

By this time, if you are skeptical about reading ahead, I am sure you will come back once again in a few days when you raise your hand in a real conference, provided you read the next 10 lines. Let the next paragraph be the last one before you quit the book, if quit is even a word in your vocabulary.

If you raised your hand without elbows slouched or bent, you most likely can skip a few chapters, if your elbow is bent or slouched, all chapters are meant for you.

At 35, having attended numerous conferences and gatherings, I have yet to witness a single person raise their hand straight upward – firm and unbending, reaching directly toward the sky, without the slightest bend at the elbow. Intrigued, I tested this myself – through repeated trials and quiet observations – before including this reflection in the pages of this book.

Question: What does a firm, unwavering hand signify?

Answer: Clarity of thought.

It is in the precision of posture that the mind often reveals its sharpest intentions.

∞

INDEX

It was my luck, fortune. Luck favors and people make it big!!!!! Period

CHAPTER 1

ABP NEWS: IDEAS OF INDIA SUMMIT 2024

22nd Feb 2024,
Bangalore airport:

I was at Terminal One, Bangalore airport, when Rudraneel texted. It was 1:00 am in Sunnyvale, he should have been sleeping by now! He enquired if I was in office. I informed him that I was about to fly to Mumbai for ABP Network's event, Ideas of India Summit 2024.

Rudraneel replied - "Oh, you are attending a live celeb event, fantastic, that is amazing. Who are the guests?"

Parul had shared with me the agenda of the event, I forwarded that to Rudraneel. He wrote, "Dr. Shashi Tharoor, Dr. Wangchuk, Aamir Khan, Omar Abdullah, you shouldn't miss them. I know you would attend Kareena Kapoor's interview and certainly all the shows anchored by Chetan Bhagat. I am excited, do share your experience later. Have an interaction with them!"

Fayez also suggested to me a couple of days ago, "Do ask a few interesting questions!"

I iterated to Rudraneel the same thing I replied to Fayez, "There is so much to learn and pick from these guys, I would prefer being silent and an absorber, wish to observe every fine detail!"

I boarded the flight, I was reading 'The Art of Management' by Shiv Shivakumar, Ex Managing Director, Nokia. Our executive program director at IIMC, Professor Chetan Joshi, had included this book in our syllabus as an impactful read to develop leadership perspective. While pursuing my Senior Management Program from IIM Calcutta, this book made a huge difference in many leading minds, including mine.

23rd Feb, 2024:

I reached Grand Hyatt, Mumbai. It was 9.40 am and the show had already begun. I had the VIP Pass, yet owing to some confusion, I had to call Parul Kamra, the then Vice President & National Sales Director, ABP Network.

Parul came rushing along with a few of her subordinates. She welcomed me with a hug and asked her subordinates to offer me her seat at the venue, in the front row and she moved ahead to meet someone in the lobby. In less than a few seconds, she came back and joined us. She wanted to ensure that I was settled well along with other peers. We entered the auditorium, she walked along with me to the front row, in front of the podium in the VIP section. A young man, reporting to Parul at work, got up the moment we reached the spot, and offered the seat to me. She asked me to settle down. Madhur Bhandarkar and other two producers whom I didn't recognize were the guests. The anchor was asking them controversial yet inquisitive questions. I always thought, celebs like them were weird and less human (media biases); prejudices of reading Page 3. Madhur Bhandarkar was an extremely simple and interesting man, who had strong perspective on many aspects of Indian politics.

In a few minutes, I saw Devendra Fadnavis, ex-CM of Maharashtra, entering the venue. He was surrounded by many guards, for a moment, I got goosebumps. He straight away walked and sat at the circular center table, where I sat. He was offered the seat to the left of mine. I was certain to step out of the table before someone asked! I was about to, when Parul came and whispered, "Shiv, even if cabinet ministers come and sit next to you, unless I tell you, you don't have to get up! You are our guest, as is anyone else. Just relax!" I had no idea how to react.

The debate between Dr. Sahasrabuddhe and Dr. Tharoor was intriguing. This was scheduled in the second half of the day. Parul was kind to hold our chairs with her colleague's help. I saw Chetan Bhagat walking and looking for a chair in the section, it was full and two of the chairs were occupied by non-celebs like me and Sanjeev. The ones with a usual pass weren't allowed into the VIP area. All chairs were full owing to this debate session. Parul, Sanjeev, and I were seated towards the right end of the region in the corner, yet front row. I looked at her while pointing out that Chetan was looking for a chair - I felt awkward occupying a chair while someone of his stature was standing, she smiled and put my arm down, asked me not to worry about it.

The debate was over in approximately 45 mins; economy, unemployment and that is it! An entire debate between BJP and Congress top leaders revolved around economy and lack of jobs. No denying that they were extremely important aspects of the countries 'present' and certainly deserved attention. I was listening and also chatting a bit with Parul, who was beside me. Famous Journalist, Vir Sanghvi was interviewing them. Unexpectedly, it appeared as if the debate was about to end; I was confused, I expected more topics to be covered. Parul, Sanjeev, and I were chatting about other things too, yet my mind was asking more from the show.

The next minute,

"I know this debate would never end, Shashi; there is a lot that you both would want to say, Dr. Sahasrabuddhe, yet, in the interest of time, I wish to open the dais for questions from the listeners, the people of India! Anyone has any questions?" Asked Vir Sanghvi.

I had an obvious question to ask, I was a Mumbaikar, 34 years old, and disappointed at the moment. I raised my hand in seconds, even Parul and Sanjeev were not expecting it. I raised a firm straight hand pointing to the roof. All fingers glued together, my reaction quick enough and with no confusion - was noticed by Dr. Tharoor. He directed Vir towards me.

Vir continued,

"Alright, Shashi says, there is a hand raised, please take the microphone, introduce yourself and ask your question!"

The microphone was right in my hand; the volunteer rushed towards me in no time.

"Hi, I am Shivratan Mishra, I work for Automated Driving.

I wish to digress from the context of employment and ask a question on the security of India!"

"Yes, go ahead," permitted Vir.

"I was born and brought up near Mumbai, and I am a 90s kid. Since our childhood, we 90s kids presumed that in every three or four years, there would be an attack in Mumbai and we must live with it. Coincidentally, since 2014 until 2024, there has been no attack in Mumbai, is this really a coincidence?" I asked.

The audience clapped and backed my question. Parul was recording me on her phone, sitting beside me. However, none of these things were on my radar while asking the question. I noticed most of it only while watching the interview Q and A several times, later.

The question I asked was not just mine, in fact it voiced the sentiments of thousands of grown-ups like me who traveled in Mumbai local trains. I remember, in July 2006, a few of my friends and I had a narrow escape from a series of 7 Bomb Blasts. This was when we all had been to Ruparel College to file our graduation application.

Those days, we did not know if there was any action or measure the government could exercise to save the fear that every Mumbaikar lived with, for a decade and more. The ruling government then was Congress, I had grown up enough to know that my intent in questioning was genuine and not to attack a particular party, it was in fact an urge to the forum, that please don't take Mumbai back to where we were more than a decade ago. 1991, 1993, 2002, 2003,

2006, 2007, 2011, if you simply Google the series of blasts in Mumbai that a 90s kid would have encountered, you will know what our psychology would be. I remember all our discussions in school, colleges, railway stations, it was only about accepting the fact that India is a democracy, we couldn't attack neighbors due to geopolitical constraints and a weak situation in J&K. We were afraid of these attacks and would count our luck periodically of how many times we missed the wrong train, factoring the right luck! No Mumbaikar would deny how suspicious we still are of every bag without an owner in a public place, even today! A few of my friends took two days to come out of their blankets when we had a narrow escape in the 2006 Borivali blasts. We left the station at 5.30 pm and at 6.15 pm, the blast blew lives. I wasn't raged, agitated, or annoyed while asking the question, it was a grown-up, pleading the opposition and ruling to not forget what we lost, keep security primal in the agenda of conversations.

Dr. Tharoor responded, "Though I would not call it a coincidence, yet it happens to coincide with the time of a weak Pakistan!......................" He continued for the next few minutes, yet he had barely much to say. Not to blame him, I respect his wisdom and capabilities, he was just representing a weaker side of the then government of India, unfortunately. He wasn't to be blamed, I am 200 percent sure, if the command was in his hands, he would have intended to save lives more than what the government did then, a financial Veteran was given a position of power where Finance was least of his problems, most of the readers understand what I mean. I nodded to his answer and being in corporate for 14 years by then, I had good listening and acceptance skills. I had to respect the human side of Dr. Tharoor, his intent was to represent the best interests of his party and people, he tried to convince through his answer. I thanked him and sat down, yet even before he could answer, it was difficult for him not to be intimidated by the reaction of the audience already. For his stature and vocabulary, I suppose simple English worked wonders, owing to the content it carried, I am being humble here!

If you are assuming in what direction the book shall go further, let me explain how this mere 2-minute conversation with Dr. Shashi Tharoor, a little accomplishment of mine had several factors falling right at one go.

How did I get the microphone? Was it a sheer coincidence?

How did I reach the venue, how and why was I invited?

How did I execute the simple conversation at a complex platform comfortably?

The strongest factor of all was, how did I get there?

It was my luck, fortune. Luck favors and people make it big!!!!! Period

Let a few of my anecdotes synchronize in the next chapters, you will see the title making sense as we move ahead.

26th Aug 2023, Kolkata:

I walked a few steps closer to Anu and whispered, "Do you really think I must perform here? A few pegs down already, these guys have forgotten they are corporate bosses!"

There were ~147 of us who enrolled together for the Senior Management Program at IIM Calcutta.

It was our convocation party; we booked an entire pub for the evening. I was a popular guitarist in the batch by now and never regretted that until this evening! The idea was to have in-house performances by internal members. A few deep literature ghazals followed by my music show. It felt like a wedding party where everyone in the audience is a quarter loaded and only wishes to dance for no reason. Sanjeev and Sharmishta presented their unique style of Ghazal and wrapped up sooner than planned, to know the crowd is not a listener anymore.

Our batch had an average 'Corporate' experience of 17 years, considering there were people of all age groups, from their 30s to early 50s. Ranging from directors of top-notch IT firms to finance experts, the batch had a mix of all genres of leaders or aspiring leaders who wanted to unlearn and relearn some basic management lessons from one of the most reputed management institutes.

Anu convinced me not to think twice and step up as per the plan. Once determined, I too didn't hesitate and walked up to the ramp and tuned my guitar and Rana's Cajon to the sound system, with the not-so-kind and helpful sound engineer at the pub. These sound engineers often don't enjoy tuning to not-so-famous performers like us. They mostly organize for celebrity performers and hence tend to undermine ordinary performers, especially like me, who aren't so famous! This human behavior is most relatable to the ones associated with corporate; you know what I mean, on a lighter note!

Rolling back my sleeves, I stepped up to the stage, held my guitar and faced the audience. Playing in front of an audience since 2014, it was my 10th or 11th on-stage performance and I knew - the little difference between a studio recording vs. live performance. You can slip a few notes here and there, however, the rhythm and beat are enough to keep the crowd engaged. I played for around 7-10 minutes and the crowd was overly engaged, humming the song along with me. I ended the performance with my own composition - Parwaah - an anecdote of my breakup back in my early 20s. As an entertainer or speaker, you must know the mood of the crowd and where to stop. On a high note, we ended the performance and opened the dance floor. I was received warmly as I stepped down and Anu affirmed, "Shiv, you killed it". Harsh bhai was right behind her and he said, "Tu sambhaal liya, amazing bro." (You handled the crowd well and the performance was amazing).

Parul congratulated me for a wonderful performance, in her style; she reminded me of my first performance at IIM C during our first campus visit. This was our second lengthy conversation getting to know each other so well.

Who knew, Parul would turn out to be a big bro friend for my life and help me climb a few healthy steps of progression with her selfless conduct and support. Let the story unfold further in the subsequent chapters.

Note :

∞

DIGITAL
EVIDENCE

I met Adil, a 23-year-old engineer, in my apartment gym—fit, focused, and employed at a prestigious multinational. He wasn't looking outward for guidance; instead, he was drawing from the wellspring within. His thoughtful questions helped crystallize many of my scattered life lessons into a cohesive vision of character. Much of what I share in this book finds its roots in those early reflections, often circling back to Chapter One.

CHAPTER 2

LEARNING A SKILL BEYOND YOUR WORK!

"You don't learn a skill; you learn about yourself while pursuing the skill. It is a path of self-discovery!"

Let's read an anecdote of my discoveries with this thought.

27 Aug 2023,
Whitefield, Bangalore,

Adil and I were walking around our apartment after an intense gym session. Adil mentioned that he saw my performance video on insta.

"How did you know that you would be able to pursue all this passion within you? When did you start learning guitar? I wish someone had taught me guitar during my childhood, I would have mastered it by now!" Claimed Adil.

"What's your age, Adil? You must be 23 as of now? I began learning guitar in 2012, I was almost your age!"

"Really?" questioned Adil.

I further explained how the guitar was an accidental discovery of a new passion. I never belonged to the school of art and music. Back in 2012, I happened to share my room with a close friend, Vijayendra Mishra. Vijju, as we called him, was given a vintage guitar by his then-girlfriend, Nikita Shah. Those days, I lived in a penthouse in Jayanagar

9th block, Bangalore. One fine evening, as I entered my room after work, I saw Vijju practicing a melody on the guitar. It was the instrumental theme of Karz movie, a tune that every beginner dreams of accomplishing. Vijju was trying his hand for the first time. It was my curious bent of mind that led me to discover and learn for the first time - how someone identifies a fret board and how to replicate a tune. Vijju asked if I wished to try. Until this point, I never knew how a beginner learns guitar, yet when someone made it so simple for me, I made it a routine to practice every evening, even spend hours trying that one tune.

I feel that I am born with almost no skill, and this perhaps is the only merit that gives me the patience to never get frustrated when I am not able to pick up something fast. I took almost a month to learn that one tune.

It was only after a few months that a friend, Jaidev Saran, visited us for a weekend. He saw the guitar in our house and instantly played 'Pani da Rang Vekh ke' song on it. For the first time, I saw someone playing chords and strumming, I was stunned. Vijju had a similar reaction. Till this point, Vijju and I were only familiar with tabs as a thing on guitar. Hearing someone play a song was just supercool. Little did we know, all his life, Jaidev only learned this one song, perhaps the sole purpose of his guitar playing was to inspire an underdog like me.

How my story turned from tabs to chords, doing small stage shows, playing Spanish freestyle Flamenco - perhaps that is a chapter for another day.

I still remember the madness of practicing 16-20 hours non-stop on my guitar over weekends. It is no surprise to any guitarist that any music instrument demands these many hours for years to let one get closer to the right frequency and vibration. Rather, let me just say that to acquire musical wisdom, there is no shortcut!

"So, learning a skill like guitar is possible at any age? What should be my takeaway from this talk?" asked Adil.

I replied, "I believe, learning a skill at any age could be possible, however I would rather quote it as, attempt to learn a skill at any age is definitely possible!"

"Did you never try to make a career in music?" asked Adil.

Guitar, as a skill, added strong content to my personality. During the process of learning this skill, I discovered a lot about myself. I learnt how to spend time alone. I experienced attention from girls after my stage performances with my band, while for ages I cried over the relationships - I barely knew, icebreaking with anyone is much easier when you have a musical trait in you. Back when I was dumped twice, if someone had told me that being a musician could save your pain of a break-up trauma, I would have aced this art years ago.

Adil probed, "So, was it all about girls back then, the main reason why you learnt the art?"

"No, it was a complimentary gain of being a musician, but my major discovery from the process of learning guitar was to discover my inner self! Every time you learn a skill, you realize the capability that your body and mind possess, and the feeling of self-sustenance gets firmer and stronger. You develop a personality that no luck or fortune can buy for you! No one ever says, I am not fit by choice, it was just luck in my favor!"

So, to conclude this learning, let's ask a question.

What did learning the guitar develop in me?

Self-sufficiency

Learning how to spend time with self

Wearing an expression of accomplishment

Musical intelligence that reflects on your personality

The above are personality traits that one experiences every time they learn or master a skill; however, there is a direct takeaway I had by learning these skills, which helped me manifest a small yet firm accomplishment of mine in 2024. I'll discuss this in the last chapter. By now, you know what I am getting at, I don't have to explain further and if you go back and read, the title of this chapter is self-explanatory.

∞

You don't just learn an art form; you discover yourself in the process!

This brings me to the next lesson and experience of life...

CHAPTER 3

IT DOESN'T MATTER HOW LESS IMPORTANT THE PROBLEM IS, SOLVE IT WITH PASSION!

Easier said than done, let's see how to make this more relatable.

20th July 2022,
Whitefield, Bangalore,

Adil enquired if I'm up for a walk after the gym session. It was after a few weeks that we timed our schedule to go to the gym together.

"How have you been, Shiv? Work keeping you busy!" Asked Adil.

"I am trying to create a roadmap for my topic and myself! I suggested to my boss if we could pitch in, to get new projects in the systems and regulatory engineering aspects expanding our Research and Development (R&D) Capabilities!" I responded.

"It's nice that you have such responsibilities to create strategies for your team! Good opportunity!" Adil sounded hopeful while saying this.

"By profile, I am the Regulation and Compliance lead for Automated Driving functions, my job role is to deliver technical stuff! I have no direct responsibility for strategy!" I replied.

"Shiv, I am unfortunately in a so-called multinational billion-dollar organization, yet my boss has no plans for my career! He doesn't have anything to say beyond the next project he would allocate to me!" Adil was sure that his career trajectory was in unsafe hands.

"Adil, I have a fill -in-the-blank question for you, 'Ratan Tata was Ratan Tata even when he was not _____ _____', you have to fill two words here!" I asked.

Adil, by now, was going to categorize me into the same pool as his boss and immediate managers. However, he was cordial enough to try, "Like, 'a professional'? I don't get it; I need your help!"

"Ratan Tata was Ratan Tata even when he was not Ratan Tata!" I claimed.

Adil was expecting more explanation for it. I continued, "The world knew Ratan Tata after his success could speak for itself; however, in his thoughts, Ratan Tata was that leader and visionary, much before the world had acknowledged him! Now, if today, we decide to make another Ratan Tata, do you think the Tata group has a formula to it?"

I helped Adil understand that *if one wishes to be extraordinary, there is no laid path towards it that someone else would know.* The best in corporate or any juncture of the world is to define one's own pathway to success unless you wish to still be ordinary. And being ordinary isn't a bad thing, in fact, only when we think and analyze, we realize that most of the people who desire to reach great heights cannot lead an ordinary life with perfection as much as an ordinary person can! The world still operates with many ordinary people doing their stuff right on a daily basis.

Be It Economy, Physics, Real Estate, Food businesses or

be it any example excluding Space exploration, if you go to the bottom of the chain, none of these areas of global operations would sustain if we don't have ordinary people doing the things right and holding the fort at the bottom of the chain. Only when you realize, it was easier for Mahatma Gandhi to be called by conception, "Father of the Nation," he couldn't ensure his son Harilal Gandhi's inclusion in his family and couldn't build a good father-son relationship. His son disowned him while the world called him 'Baapuji'! In simple and direct terms, it's easier to be a Godly figure than 'being human' and sustaining a strong family and daily life construct, certainly wearing a T-shirt with the caption is a different thing!

Someone who clearly wishes to be ambitious and strives to achieve something huge in his or her life, cannot expect his boss to lay out the roadmap for them. Bosses may plan a roadmap to make you an ordinary person in the industry based on his or her sample size of growth seen so far with their experience. If you ask a pilot the best way to reach Jaipur from Bangalore, he/she would in a fraction of second recommend a flight, a railway train driver would propose a train first and quote flight as an option with an included cost while an Ola intercity Cab driver would also recommend an alternate as you might have guessed. The rest is self-explanatory.

"What if I believe and know that I am much better than my manager, I can do his job better than he does! I don't see why he is in his position!" Asked Adil.

I wasn't surprised, every skilled young professional goes through this phase once in life when it is difficult to find content in their superiors. Brings the next chapter of the book, "I know I am better than my boss!"

∞

If one wishes to be extraordinary there is no laid path towards it that someone else would know.

CHAPTER 4

I KNOW I AM BETTER THAN MY BOSS!

"Adil, have you driven a four-wheeler before?" I asked.

"Yes, I have. However, I have not been good at it, need road experience!" responded Adil.

"Do you really think driving is a rare skill? If not, then why don't you know it?" I probed further.

Adil was feeling slightly under check, however, he continued to respond, "I haven't tried and focused on driving yet!"

"Are you aware that the average urban crowd files their driving license request between the age of 18 to 25 years?" I continued.

"Yeah, that makes sense," responded Adil. "How is this related to the context we are discussing now? I am sure it does, however, I'm curious!" Adil inquired with genuine interest.

"A major reason why we end up learning to drive in this age bracket and the official age bracket for license application, is due to a few factors: many families are able to buy a car only from their daughter's/son's first salary; there is prioritization of learning to drive car only after your first job." I informed.

"Your boss isn't sitting at that position owing to his expertise alone or because he is better than you at the skill, more often than not, it is about knowing how to drive the show or the project, which only comes at a certain age and experience!" Period. I explained.

"You mean to say, there aren't incompetent people in higher positions in the corporate?" asked Adil.

"No, I am rather saying that he is better than you to run the show as of today, else the show would have collapsed. Moreover, you can be a great coder, yet you won't be able to turn on the Coffee machine in your cafeteria with the same efficacy as the experienced staff in your pantry, even with a fully guided user manual!" I suggested. Most positions are filled based on skill, yet served on the basis of muscle memory & reflexes, these are two key hallmarks of experience in any domain.

The conversation continued as I convinced Adil that an industry doesn't run on experts at all levels. Intelligence is a mediocre word based on the evaluator judging you over your imaginative skills or analytical skills! More than often, a person who answers 2+2/2 = 2 might in fact be sitting in higher positions in Corporate and delivering better results, while for a smart Mathematician, someone answering it as 2 is not competent! What's important to know is that even in the norm, once you remind the person about BODMAS and the other person comprehends it after an explanation, is equally intelligent or differently intelligent compared to the latter.

P.S:

Coincidentally, Adil gifted me a book titled 'Outlier' on my birthday in 2024 this year, and somewhere in the book, it talks at length about distinct aspects of intelligence.

I believe, by this juncture, you must have connected well to the book. Now I can portray areas where Adil and my conversation becomes a mutual learning for both of us. I'll skip the anecdotes and discontinue the direct speech from here on to focus on the content and not the context.

The below chapters have been extrapolated from my discussions at length with Preetysh, Fayez and Adil.

∞

CHAPTER 5

DISCIPLINE OF COMMITMENT VS DISCIPLINE OF TIME!

The chapter title would show an alternate definition of discipline, which I have learnt over the course of many years. Be it fitness, diet, work, or life goals.

This chapter is more essential for those who often struggle to reach their workplace on time yet are committed to their job; those who often reach late for a date are not yet betrayers; those who often don't compliment yet love most sincerely and others are those who just don't know how to reach on time, period

I have an answer on Quora over my 'Fat to Fit Journey' which has over a hundred thousand views, not because my answer is that great, but because the question is so popular! I have a lot of unpleasant things to share when it comes to my past health experiences, however, I chose to rather quote, 'today, I am one of the sturdiest individuals around me; not the best though when it comes to pull-ups, push-ups, arm wrestling, single arm push-ups, pistol squats and endurance swimming, which I began learning when I was 29.'

I wish to talk about the significance of workouts to an individual's development in corporate life, personal life, relationships and mental health. I'll explain an example of each, bit by bit, how that helps at the core.

27 Nov' 22:

I was returning from Kolkata to Bangalore after my one-week campus immersion at IIMC. As already mentioned in the previous chapters, I had enrolled for the Senior Management Program at IIM Calcutta. We were the 19th batch, and this course was offered to eligible candidates who have served at least 10 years in the industry. There will be another chapter stating more about my course, but for now, I'll tell you about my ice-breaker with the air hostess of a popular airline. Before I move to the below conversation, I must share that I have been an average-looking guy for all my life. I had never received compliments about my looks until I was 33 years old. It all began after I invested a few years in muscle training and clean eating. I wish to hint, that for any individual to get to his/her best (no matter how good you are, the best of you needs more effort) form of appearance, needs to invest time in physical workout sessions - be it yoga, gym or sports. Additionally, one must have a good, affordable tailor. The brand you wear doesn't matter as much as how you wear it. Beer Biceps had a huge influence on my life when it came to building a strong appearance. Back in 2017, I used to follow his channel and learn about clothing, grooming and everything that a man is deprived of in our society, to know by direct means.

"Sir, do you need some water?" The air hostess asked. I was reading. I nodded and took the glass offered to me.

"Sir, don't mind, however, let me ask you, I can clearly recognize you to be someone I have seen on TV!" She stooped down, I could see her smiling cheek beneath the mask!

"Do you think I am the elder brother of the lead character in Ekta Kapoor's series? No Ma'am, I am not that old!" I replied.

She immediately corrected and, by choice and interest on both sides, prolonged the conversation. I could go on to narrate the conversation, but the book is not a romantic series penned by Nicholas Spark.

"Today is my 7th marriage anniversary! You are cute, thank you for letting me feel appreciated, yet the cutest of my life is waiting at the airport, with a cake in her hand to celebrate, as soon as I land!" My witty self remarked.

She blushed and made a sad yet funny face and said, "You are adorable, I am heartbroken yet am glad we spoke!"

I told her, "All my life I would have waited for this moment to be true, and just when for a decade I gave up and focused on my own thing, I see the marvel happening!"

Presently, she is a good friend, and we have been connected on Instagram since then.

I eventually inferred how a few factors listed below could make you someone's...... oh wait, an Air Hostess's crush.....

Factors:

Jaw line + Formal attire + Armani Shirt + A good book + and an attitude of not being attentive to the world unless necessary!

I always wondered if a jaw line was nature's bliss; however, if I can have it, trust me, anyone in the world can have better. It is a thing associated with muscle training, in the right form and organic progression.

I can perhaps write a book on fitness and how to begin with it etcetera. However, in the digital world, I am sure most of us can find out the means of knowing best exercise practices and so on. Let me address few basic parameters that might help tweak your brain to comprehend the constraints holding you from hitting the gym or perhaps staying consistent.

Time management?

You mostly do not have constraints with regards to time, 20-minute workout on alternate days is sufficient to bring in good change in your physique, in 3 to 6 months. If you are reading this book, then you must set aside 20 minutes off your schedule, thrice a week, of course, once you are done reading!

The fundamental issue is 'Mood Switching'! This advances us to the next chapter.

∞

DIGITAL
EVIDENCE

CHAPTER 6

MOOD SWITCHING

Imagine being exhausted the entire day at your corporate office. Once you reach home, imagine a scenario where you have to pad up to meet your crush vs. where you have to pad up to meet your fiancé's parents! One sounds exciting and you might have all the world's energy to get your ass moving vs. the other sounds dissipating and most likely you would need to push yourself real hard to make it. The only difference is the mood! ***Your mind could do anything if it knows that your mood gets enhanced and better by the next activity, the time lapse can be a real thing!***

If your subconscious mind can process the mood before pursuing an activity, your mind knows exactly if this is worth it or not. The mood itself drives you to the next task.

If you can master the art of hacking your mood, you can do any task, including cleaning utensils with 100% interest. Next time, when you or your colleague talk about time being a problem for not being able to stay consistent at your workout, help the forum know it is more than often mood instead of time which is the real culprit.

A simple way to kickstart your workout routine is by identifying the least resistance goal of fitness.

I had seen a video of finger push-ups by someone on the internet, I wanted to master this art. I used a simple hack; I began opening every push door at work without touching my palm, just with all 5 fingers. To make it more productive, I ended up opening the door from the hinge side, which isn't easy and needs more contact. Would you believe if I tell you, just by opening my office washroom door for a few months with my fingers on the hinge side, I can do a few good form pushups on my fingers any day, anytime (provided, I already was able to do normal pushups, stay there).

Fitness and strength training is simple if you understand the art. I have observed, small-scale 'wall whitewash painters' have well-defined shoulder muscles. They would for years just rub the brush against the wall for 1000 iterations and would never need to lift weights to have that lean mass. Now, if you go back to the Karate Kid movie, you will know why simple hand movements done for iterations and hours, either the same day or across the year, can develop the muscles to be relatively strong. Muscle building is an art, it needs to be organic and easy on your mind and body, so be a painter and not an over-exaggerated, aggressive weightlifter, of course, if you aren't into championships. If you have any doubts about this theory not working, I'll share my Insta handle at the end of the book (I am not an influencer nor have many followers), feel free to see what my body tone is like! I have barely lifted 5-7 kg dumbbells till now for 6 years, yet I have a fine-tuned body by methodically practicing the art form. If any of your gym friend tells you that the method of low weight and organic muscle building without lifting heavy isn't the true method, it doesn't work; well don't care about his bicep size, message me on my Insta handle and ask that person to fly to Bangalore and do arm wrestling with me for 60 seconds. A 2.5 kg dumbbell with right form can give you much more strength than 15 kg with bad form.

I wish to narrate a small story about my fitness journey and the impact on me by this one man, Jitendra Chouksey! FITTR company, which is now funded by several top Entrepreneurs of India, made a huge impact on my fitness journey when I began in Jan 2019.

24th Dec, 2018:

I was 81 kgs with two episodes of Slip Disc, four screws in my right shoulder, a Pilonoidal Sinus surgery and by this time I had recovered from a critical Health condition - G B Syndrome. G B S is a rare occurrence that happens to one in one million. All these health issues remained with me from 2009-2018. I could neither workout, nor lift a laptop weighing 3 kgs! I was the same guy who was one of most aggressive sports freaks until college life. I wasn't the best yet I was extremely passionate. However, life brought me full circle, slouching on my breakfast chair at work, with a paunch and a stiff back.

'I know I have tried several times in past years and failed, yet someday I too should be able to have six packs! Maybe that might happen, who knows!' I ended up thinking aloud. Rahul, Ritesh, and I were having breakfast together at the office. We were 10 days old in one of the top-notch global car-makers which had a legacy of 100+ years of dominance in the European and global market.

'Mishraji, you are an 'uncle', people at your age plan kids, not six packs!' Ritesh was a young chap, and we had a habit of always being sarcastic with each other. We became friends since the day we joined the new firm together. I was determined to give an attempt to working out again, I tried for 9 years and failed every time, however, the stories of cricket players overcoming several injuries was my way of not losing hope. Knowing that nothing is impossible, I took a bet with Ritesh. 'One year from today, on 24th Dec 2019, I'll have six pack abs, I don't know how, yet I am sure I will!' I said with resolve. He laughed and I claimed that I'm serious. The price of the bet was to treat the group in a five-star fine-dining place. Frankly, I was sure Ritesh was on the winning side of the bet. Other than the fact that I have strong willpower and conviction, I had no logic by my side to back my resolve!

I had managed to get a rental accommodation at Prestige Shantiniketan, Whitefield, Bangalore. Two days had passed since the bet and I was totally clueless on where to begin. At that time, I believed in the stereotypical theory of working out - lifting heavy weights, and so on.

Knowing your limits is the biggest asset a human being can have. I knew I could lift 2 kgs and not more, even a 3 kgs laptop ruins my right shoulder, owing to the screws and multiple surgeries I had gone through. I was passing by the parking lobby of my apartment tower 21 when I saw a daily wage worker painting the wall. I saw his lean defined shoulders and went for a small talk. 'Bhaiya, yeh shoulder kaise banaya? Gym jaate ho kya?', (Brother, how did you build your lean shoulder muscles? Do you also workout?) I enquired.

He smiled and responded, "Bhaiya, brush hi uthate hain daily, diwaar pe ragaddte hain, bas yehi apna borkout hai!" (Brother, I just pick the brush daily and paint the wall, that's my workout.) He would perhaps be from UP or Bihar as per his accent, he didn't pronounce the word workout right yet made a revelation which was the most expensive thing I learnt from him that evening.

I immediately rushed to Decathlon near Phoenix Mall and bought a pair of 2 kg dumbbells. I decided to use the dumbbell like the painter would use his brush.

Every day after work, be it night 10 pm or evening 7 pm, I ensured to work out an hour or more with the 2 kg dumbbells. I had to travel to Chennai every weekend since my wife stayed there in a hotel. She was working for a multinational pharmaceutical firm. I barely knew anything about diet and hence by the usual stereotype, I ended up removing carbs entirely from my diet and fixed myself to 8 egg whites and 100 gms of paneer every night. I didn't even know the significance of protein in diet etc., with my half-baked knowledge, I remained consistent with the process.

"Half knowledge is dangerous only if you do not know the remaining half exists!"

What I loved about myself was that I was constantly trying to explore and learn more about fitness from every Tom, Dick and Harry who had something to say. I never believed

100 percent in what I was doing, yet kept validating better methods to reach my goal. Every day with the 2 kg dumbbells, I would perform all body workouts I ever knew or saw on YouTube. At 29, you develop patience in life, you know things take time and you aren't warm-blooded anymore. I knew that I couldn't afford another injury and hence I began a very moderate, low-intensity workout with the dumbbells for the first two weeks. I was afraid of shoulder dislocation with 2 kg dumbbells, I knew I was fragile, yet there was something in me that wanted to win the bet. I wanted to do it once so that everyone in the world could believe that there is a return from the damages and injuries. After the first three weeks, 2 kgs felt lighter.

My workout intensity extended to below counts:

Biceps curl: 50-60 reps x 2 kg dumbbells x 5 sets

Triceps extensions: 20-30 reps x 2kg dumbbells x 4 sets

Shoulders: I used to write alphabets in the air with the dumbbell to train the shoulder muscles functionally.

Days passed and I continued my efforts with 2 kg dumbbells and in my mind almost accepted that this might not really make much difference. Still, I could feel that holding my laptop bag was no longer a problem, in fact, I was able to open my car door easily. I was able to raise my right arm above my shoulder without any pain. I knew abs were nowhere visible nor was I able to lift more weights, maybe I was scared, I had to be! I didn't know if the painter's theory would ever work, yet I didn't have a better choice!

April, 2019:

One fine afternoon on a Saturday, I decided to stay back in Bangalore and not visit my wife since I had some other priorities aligned and she understood it well. I entered the lift and stepped to the rear wall beside an elderly man who was whistling Rajesh Khanna songs. He suddenly looked up at me and asked, "Beta gym jaate ho na? Bahot fit ho, hamare zamane mein hamein pata hi nahin tha warna mein bhi aaj is umar mein Dara Singh jaisa fit hota, pata hai ab to chalne firne mein bhi dikkat hoti hai!'('Son, do you go to the gym regularly? You are really fit; we weren't aware much about fitness during our young age, else I would have also been fit like Dara Singh at this age. You know, now walking upright also seems like pain.')

I smiled and thanked him for the compliment. I informed that I work out at home, and do not visit any gym.

I went home straight into my room, stood beside the dumbbells, took off my T-shirt, and looked at myself. Eureka moment!!!!!! It was working, it did. I was never the guy who would be seen fit, to be quoted as an example. I couldn't believe it! A small accomplishment, yet it felt like something was right about the way I was thinking and executing. It made sense and I was getting there. I was emotional, I was certain, I knew I had a few more months to go, I knew it was hard, I knew I might win, I knew almost everything from now is possible, but one step at a time. I took the next big step!!!!! Guess what???????

I bought 3 kg dumbbells! If you were expecting anything big or huge, like hitting the commercial gym, getting six-pack abs or anything else, unfortunately, this book won't jump pages of life, I am going to break every step organically and make sense of it at the end. You would see how achieving everything is simplest in its form, if taken one step at a time!

I don't struggle with discipline or aim to achieve perfection, I thrive to achieve a little thing which is profound, I call it 'figuring out'!

A popular podcaster whom I follow judiciously is Raj Shamani. I stumbled upon his YouTube channel by accident and the name of his channel, 'figuring out' resonated with my belief system! I knew exactly what would keep me tuned to his channel and be his subscriber; it's his channel's name! What I learn from the channel is an echo of the term, figuring out!

∞

Half knowledge is dangerous only if you do not know the remaining half exists.

CHAPTER 7

FEAR & FIGURING OUT!

This chapter is the most essential content for the majority of us dealing with the real world as humans. It helps us understand not just the concept of 'confidence', rather the concept of confidence in adversity, during lack of power and money, confidence while you are an underdog!

Facing your fear is a critical aspect of human existence. If you are an animal, you don't have a choice. The fear of being killed is real; the fear of a deer being chased by a leopard and a lion being hunted by humans is a real thing. You are born to live with fear. A deer runs, a snake retaliates, a lion attacks, all of them face their fear while we humans are taught to feel that safe space is for 'real'! We are tuned to believe that the world must be a safe space. The instincts and intuitions of observing your surroundings with suspicion - raises your cortisol and isn't an acceptable form of the world we live in. Ever thought if animals go through a higher level of stress hormones when they feel endangered? To make the book more effective or reading-ready I certainly could browse and find out research papers on animals' stress levels when under an attack, yet I didn't do any of that. All I wish to bring to your notice is the fact that being in fear is perhaps normal in their existence, they maintain the state of calm around the fear and that is an art every human being must master. This perhaps, is the only definition of alpha male I believe could ever make real sense. Interestingly, you do not have to be a male to be an alpha male, it is independent of your gender!

2nd Aug, 2007,
Alandi, Pune:

I was in the second year of Engineering. I studied in one of the most reputed colleges of Pune, Maharashtra. Our branch was situated in a small village near Pune called Alandi. I was a popular and extrovert college boy, dating a girl who was the daughter of the then Assistant Commissioner of Police, Pune urban. Our college was extremely political, however, that is a story for another book! Let me narrate a small encounter that changed a lot, in my experience of myself and the world around me. I was seventeen and a half on this day.

Around 11.30 pm, my friend Abhinav and I were walking back to our hostel when Abhinav took a break to collect his notes from Naveen (we called him Ganja (bald) for obvious reasons). I was waiting outside Amritwani hostel, the place where Naveen stayed. This hostel had mostly seniors and super seniors staying for ages. Super seniors still in college were the ones who took 6 plus years to complete their engineering. Today, there are extremely successful people from our university who would have completed engineering in 10+ years as well. Years of completion defined nothing of a person's caliber or skill, it certainly depicted the discipline aspect in the worldly definition.

A couple of Seniors from the neighboring room sneaked out as they heard my voice talking to Abhinav. Vipul Bashisht, called me inside his room. I said, 'Sir, Ghar Jaa raha hun, Abhinav ka wait kar raha hun!', I informed him that I am waiting for Abhinav, and then we are headed home shortly. He insisted that I come inside, a bit assertively this time! He was drunk, I entered, and they locked the door.

"Drink this!" He commanded.

"Sir, mein daaru nehin peeta!", I told him that I avoid alcohol.

"Tu sirf bhaashan deta hai, Sabkee problem solve karta hai! G****, pee!" Malik Vyapari abused me and claimed that I consider and claim to be an Orator and problem solver, I must drink without an excuse.

The door was locked, and they were drunk enough that any further negation could have consequences. At least in my mind, yes! I tried to request, used the word please and almost begged, joining my hands. I was not even sure why the ones who don't even know me directly are targeting me. This moment felt like ages, the room felt like a cage, I could only think of a stronger me who never had to beg ever before this moment. Speaking on stage and being assertive was easier; this moment was tough, real tough!

The 17-year-old me was unable to accept the defeat, I kept trying but then I had to give up. I drank whatever was in the bottle, it had no label. There were so many bottles of cold drinks and Whiskey. I took a sip and could barely understand what it was. Once done, I kept the bottle back and they asked me to leave the room.

I left the room. I was fine and normal, just silent. I didn't know what just happened. Abhinav saw me and asked, "Bhai kidhar chala gaya tha? Kya bol raha tha b*** ka l****, Vipul! Ragging lee kya teri? Tu chup kyun hai!" Abhinav enquired if I was fine and was curious to know what happened inside the room. My mother was in my thoughts while walking, she hated people who drink mainly because people lose control over their senses, and it makes them do things their sane self would never want to; I was all in tears. I couldn't walk straight, it was owing to the humiliation and not alcohol, felt drunk by force, felt like a loser! I was trying to console myself that it might have been a soft drink, yet it reminded me of all the helpless situations and people I have watched in movies or experienced around me. Ragging was a popular practice in our college, yet it was never beyond conversations or verbal intimidation. The idea was to build a hierarchy, kill the ego of newcomers, keep minds grounded and support decorum during elections. Elections were a massive thing in our college, in fact much more important than exams.

Forcing someone to drink anything wasn't a normal practice in ragging, it is not a normal practice anywhere in the world, be it anything. Controlling anyone's life, food, drinks, choices, even if it's your sibling or spouse, is a clear question to one's freedom of livelihood and expression. An acquaintance here crossed all sorts of lines, the realization was dawning on me while I kept walking. By the time we reached our apartment, my expressions were enough for anyone to figure out I wasn't sane; I had lost my confidence entirely. In no time, entire apartment's friends stepped down and were outraged by this event. Morya Vihar apartment had limited flats and all of them were my close friends. We stayed more than a year together, it was our second year and by this time we were brothers, and everyone knew I did not consume alcohol. In no time, the rage reached Patna Hostel, another PG where most of our friends from Bihar stayed. The ecosystem was so Bihar-friendly there, in terms of studies, food culture, discussion on politics etc., that the PG was default named for itself!

It was 11.40 pm, dark and quiet, the crowd signified unrest and loud disturbance, we began marching towards Amritwani hostel. Another ten mins, by 11.50 pm, altogether 40 of us gathered at Amritwani. There were a few prominent names that led the group, yet the front runner was Dhiraj Shahi. Shahi was thin, small, tiny and had a mustache. In an ideal world, Shahi should be afraid of anyone if it were about physical ability, yet in Shahi's world, he was fearless!

"Kaun tha, Shivratan? Yeh tha? Bolo M***** ko gaad denge!" (Shivratan, tell me who it was? Was this the guy? Tell me now, I will ensure he doesn't see the next morning). Shahi pointed at a senior whom I had barely seen. I was not even sure to reply and was trying to draft my response. Within no time, Shahi slapped the same guy as he tried countering Shahi for pointing at him! "Humko sawaal mat punch, chup chap khade reh, abhi hamara dimaag out hai," (Don't ask me questions, stand quietly, I am not in my senses right now) said Shahi! The senior was not at fault, yet he knew the emotions and risk in case he retaliates - it was a crowd of 40 fearless angry youngsters. The senior decided to refrain from speaking anything else and by this time many local and Bihari seniors staying in Amritwani stepped in to moderate, the seniors who would have ragged us and had huge respect from us after the ice breaker a year ago, now were afraid to poke us much. Holding deep breaths, they were trying to moderate the situation. I pointed out Vipul's door, the same room where I was held and forced to drink. The door was shut, I had to point out else Shahi would have hit a few more non-related people there in his rage.

By this time, Preet Ranjan and a few others were already off their mind and warmed up enough that they banged the door hard and screamed the names of the same seniors who ragged me a while ago. Malik opened the door in half sleep, he was a fat chap with long hair. He had no clue about the rage on the other end of his closed door. The moment he opened the door and asked what was happening, he got slapped multiple times and it was difficult to recognize whose hands they were. Everyone jumped onto him and dragged him to his bed and loaded punches, chairs, and everything that people could grab. Malik was crying and shouting, he could see the fear of dying, he was scared. Few of us tried searching for Vipul, but we could not see any trace of him. After almost 10 minutes of thrashing, Malik was begging to be saved from death. Someone pulled me in front of his face and asked him to apologize! "Bhai, save me, please!" wept Malik. Seeing him in that state was a role reversal in the shortest span anyone would have ever imagined! I could see the same fear and helplessness in him. I looked into his eyes and pointed fingers towards his face and said, "Mein daaru nehin peeta, I don't consume alcohol, don't dare to force me ever again!" I cried a lot, uttering those words in rage. I could not still hit him, yet some part of my fear had taken a back seat. I could for the first time ever, since I was born, notice a person who showed anger, rage, overconfidence, fearlessness - knocked down and begging for life!

This moment made me realize, there is no one with absolute power in the world; it is always relative to the state of mind of the person in front of you!

We left the room and walked up to the college front gate. This was our 'open roof den', Alandi being a small village near Pune, Police patrolling wasn't prominent, and we college students used to face them often with no fear, owing to the age we were in, you barely think so much.

I am not proud of what happened that night, I feel bad for Malik, for others who got beaten without their fault, yet I can mention that none of us including Malik or Shahi were criminals or bad people, we were just operating on our reflexes without understanding the consequences on others and ourselves. I can't change the past nor feel afraid to accept it, instead I can apologize to Malik for all he went through, it was not intended! This narrative is in the spirit of the chapter. Today, I do not regret any of the incidents that happened to me because what I am is a product of all these experiences, and trust me, I am fearless and empathetic much more than I was that day!

Coming back to the story, it is not over — in fact, that revenge was barely anything in front of what we and especially I went through in the next six months after this incident. Let me narrate what happened at 1:00 am the same night.

We were now winners, celebrating our success, self-belief and arrogance were confused terms for us. Everyone was on top of their confidence, we felt like warriors, dominating goons, kings, on top of the world. After all the celebrations, we ended up heading back home, like usual, I went along with the Bihari gang to Patna hostel. We were analyzing the whole incident, and I was smiling in confidence and sense of accomplishment when we received a call from HP Sir who informed us that Malik has been taken to police station where they are filing a half murder case as Malik's face was bleeding badly, he could have lost an eye may be! Hitanshu Parekh, also referred to as HP Sir, was a senior we feared the most, yet after the ragging icebreaker, he became our close friend. We were appreciated and loved by all the backbencher seniors who had control over college politics and dynamics outside studies, they still were figuring out life inside college, and had strong resilience to life outside college premises!

"Sir, ab kya karein? Daaru toh wahi pilaya tha." (Sir, what should we do now? He was the one who forced Shiv to drink, claimed Ranjan.)

"Tum log abhi neeche aao aur college ke pass saare milo, Malik ke pass jake hum log solve karlenge!" suggested HP Sir. He proposed to meet near college right this hour and he would moderate the differences. Immediately as an instant reaction, 20+ of us rushed towards college on our feet, leaving behind our bikes at home. We reached mid-way when we saw Kapse Sir, Sujan Sir and HP Sir walking or in fact running toward us. By now we knew they were not going to help, we tried to slow them down, yet it was too late.

"Tum log don ban gaye ho college kya! (Are you guys the new rulers of the college!)" HP Sir held Preet Ranjan, Sujan Sir held Jolly and Kapse Sir held Trivedi, they began thrashing them. I also remember Sujan Sir hitting Jolly with a small stone in his hand. It wasn't that we couldn't hit them back, but we were frozen. We had no clue since these seniors loved us until the day before. Respect, fear and lack of reflexes held us back. Trivedi, Preet and Jolly also knew well that reacting wasn't the best as we didn't know how many more were on their way. Let me also share, Trivedi, who I am referring to in the story, is a popular Actor from TVF. Trivedi was a strong personality on his intellectual and fearless side. He was exactly like the character, as he appears in his Amazon series which I wish not to reveal. He is a star now and associated with TVF, I am apprehensive to mention his name here without consensus.

Knowing his popularity even during our college days, he

ended up being the target on this day, seniors targeted the strong and bold personalities first, the three I named were in the obvious list. None of the three were afraid, they were facing it boldly and trying to explain. There was no fear, there was eye contact without rage. Trivedi, Jolly and Preet knew they could handle it but hitting back could be the last nail in the coffin of what we had welcomed. In these few minutes, we knew we had entered an unknown tunnel.

We all decided to run as we were unaware of how many more were coming. Sonali, my then-girlfriend, along with other girls, were on their hostel terrace watching the whole scenario. Sonali had a personal interest, but obvious, I had updated her on everything happening there - real time. We ran enough to reach Patna Hostel entry when someone suggested, let us go to the hilltop and stay in the jungle, else people can also come to our home and thrash. Everyone at once stepped to the hilltop and we rested there for an hour, closely watching the streets. I can see the events live as I am narrating here, the memory isn't vague at all, it's crystal clear even today, while I am drafting the story after 16 years. The entire night we spent in two rooms, having absolutely no clue what the morning would be like.

By 7 am, someone knocked on my door and woke me up, as I looked down the gallery, 100+ seniors, locals, and 30+ bikes were waiting downstairs to pick all of us up. We couldn't believe this; we didn't know half of them. We were clueless, wondering what was happening. Malik was a super senior, in fact, from 2001 batch who spent more than 7 years in the college already, yet figuring out his final year. Malik was senior to HP, Sujan, and many others, hence close to them. It was surprising that we never knew this. We would have done the same thing no matter what, since we were running on our reflexes, not our calculated actions. It takes years to master this one art, and some of us barely achieve it!

We were fortunate that Patna Hostel's landlord, who was a family person, strictly warned everyone downstairs not to dare get into his apartment. He asked them to do anything and everything they wish to outside his house and not there! Although they were angry and justified, yet they knew their boundaries; no one was a criminal, no one would enter a family man's apartment and do things that disturb the harmony and mental health of the family. Moreover, there is always a fear of the unknown and most of the guys standing outside knew the landlord is also a local guy and can come back strong at them.

All friends, including me, went back to our rooms when Kartik Niwas Choubey Sir visited us. Kartik Niwas Choubey was our immediate senior, never got into college politics, yet always delivered fearless eye contact to anyone he encountered. Never ragged nor argued, he would look into the eyes of seniors and say, "Dekhiye, humko aapse koi lena dena nehin hai, humko mat ghasitiye!" ("I don't have any business with you, don't bother me!") He was never troubled by anyone till this day.

He entered our room; I met him for the first time.

"Sir, ragging woh liya, daaru woh pilaa raha tha aur ab

humko kyun sab log bol rahe hain ke marenge?" translated as, "Sir, he ragged us, forced us to drink, why are we under threat?" Asked Preet Ranjan.

"Bahot maardiye ho usko, super senior hai aur uska chehra dekhake kisi ko baki baton pe wishwas hi nehin ho raha! Baki aadmi apna hawaa karega kyunki election mein sabko GS, CS banana hai. Abhi maamla gambhir hai, yahanse nikalna mushkil hai kuch din!" He explained to us the exact situation in a short span. He informed us that the injuries on Malik's face were enough to rage other seniors, he also stated how many other seniors want to showcase their power and find this as an opportunity.

I was scared by now; life wasn't going to be normal again. We all regretted it; I was wondering how the guys who showed too much confidence last night were all hiding behind the doors. Preet, Trivedi, Jolly were bold and calm, yet Bhaskar Murali, who was always our leader and considered to be the fearless one, was not even coming out of his house, hiding like a coward. I was analyzing everything, for the first time I realized that not everything people say should be believed, not everyone who says he/she is fearless – actually is, not everyone who is tiny and small has to be afraid and moreover, on a weak day and a weak moment, anyone can come and manhandle you or at least threaten you over phone just like we were getting calls from random numbers by now.

My father called. He had a fair idea of the situation since last night 1 am. He knew I was hiding around the hills, and yet for some reason, he was calm and asked me to call in the morning.

"How is the situation there? All ok?" He enquired!

"Papa, we are not going out of the house, I am here, and it is fine but 100+ people are looking for us, six of us especially are on the list!" I answered a bit anxiously, yet he was calm, despite knowing what I was going through. You see, calmness radiates too.

He asked me, "Can you handle it, or do you want me to come there?"

"I will handle it Papa, I will call you if I am unable to." I replied. Exactly 1.5 years back when he came to enroll me to the college, he was in tears seeing me being alone, he did not know how I'll handle myself and my life, yet this day he acted like a mentor, he was delivering such trust when I was in the middle of a life threat situation!

I kept the phone down and, in a few minutes, I called Avdhesh Karve Sir. Back in 2006, when I had come for my admission, my father contacted Karve Sir. Via random network, Karve got me accommodation in Morya Vihar Apartment. Karve was a strong personality and had strong connections, yet owing to multiple backlogs and lost years, he had exited college. I called him and explained everything. He called me back in a few minutes,

"Would you trust my recommendation?" He asked!

"Haan Sir, ab face karna hai!" I affirmed that I trust him!

"HP ayega, tujhe bike pe leke jayega, mere pe bharosa rakh,

mein wahan nehin hun par meri guarantee hai ke tereko kuch nehin hoga!" He confirmed that HP sir shall pick me up and take me out, he assured my security and asked me not to be afraid.

I agreed and came back to the room, informing my friends that HP Sir would come and pick me up. My friends kept recommending that I rather not trust anyone, and it could be a trap, yet I knew at some point that I was tired of being scared, sitting in the room, and waiting! I don't know how, yet fear had taken a backseat even though I knew I was risking my life and career, both. Sonali was aware and she was at her hostel balcony watching everything live in front gate of our college. Her hostel was right beside the college entrance. She informed me that HP Sir left on his bike and around 100 people are still there in the front gate area, at the cafe.

I received a call from HP in a few minutes, "Shivratan, neeche aa!" He asked me to come downstairs.

Preet Ranjan, Shahi, Kartik Niwas Choubey warned me not to go, I decided to face it, I realized that the fear is slowly fading away, and the situation became the new normal for me.

I would pause this story and share a quick minute of events that happened in chronological order over the next six months starting from this day,

HP Sir took me for a face-off with everyone, where I met all the outraged seniors.

I managed to negotiate that we all come to the college entrance and ask for forgiveness.

A common senior friend who stayed in Patna hostel, Mridul, gave the alternate contact of a local corporator's (elected member) friend who can back us up, and suggested that we avoid apologizing and face off!

I suggested friends not to involve local goons.

Ego won over wisdom; we ended up seeking the support of a local corporator's friend.

The local Corporator's friend came with us, and we all marched to the college gate.

The moment we reached, this guy, without asking anything, broke two chairs on HP and Sujan.

HP and Sujan ran to their safety.

Other seniors also left without a second thought.

Akash Bhat Sir, one of the most fearless seniors, didn't move an inch and no one dared to touch him, nor he touched anyone; he just said one thing, "You guys got locals into college politics, now this won't end here! This is a trap; you all would fall into soon!"

Eventually, two months after this episode, Shyam, the Corporator's friend extorted money from me. He did not know much beyond the fact that he helped me in crisis. I tried seeking help from multiple friends to get me out of the situation, yet no one could help. Mridul Gupta, the senior who got Shyam into the whole story, himself could not handle him later.

It took me six months to come out of this situation and 1.5 years to teach Shyam his lesson for life, so that he would never extort money from anyone. Shyam is even today not allowed to step into Alandi premises, he barely knew he was digging his own grave.

By the time I left college, I was a student leader, doing election campaigning for local MLAs, 40 of us, who joined hands to hit Malik that night, were no longer good friends. We were fragmented into smaller groups.

I can author a whole book on every step taken by me during these two years. However, the most significant role played by someone in this whole episode, which changed my entire way of looking at the world, was by my mother, Aruna Devi.

To give you a brief about her background - Aruna Devi managed to finish her class 7 studies, which was considered matriculation back in 70s. Her village did not have a school offering education beyond that. Her father, my grandpa, wanted her to study further; however, she just needed one more woman's company back in time since commuting to the city alone for a girl in the remote village of Darbhanga, Bihar, wasn't an easy and safe deal. Getting back to the point about my mother's role.

Interestingly, 'How to raise a child' is still not a book in schools, yet parents manage to outperform this task without a structured education about it. In fact, I am glad the current generation of schools do not teach this, else they would inherently force competitiveness within parents' minds too! Peer pressure in the primitive world was only about who gets more meat after a hunt, now in the current era, the entire education system instills peer pressure at every stage of their kids' lives. I was raised differently. Instead of asking to stay safe and not risk my life, my mother had a different perspective and suggestion, thanks to her, it changed my attitude for this life as I faced the world of threats and discomfort. Let's find out more in the subsequent chapter.

Ever in life if you struggle to make eye contact with anyone, be it your boss, your company's CEO, your country's top officials, a cop, a criminal, your country's Prime Minister; the below chapter shall help you overcome; the chapter shall have no title, you can define the title after reading!

∞

CHAPTER 8

THE ONE WITH NO TITLE

1st Oct 2007, Boisar, Thane, Near Mumbai:

I returned home after spending over a month resolving the entire conflict. This was before the extortion calls by Shyam, just the time when the back-and-forth threats had stopped.

I reached home around 8:50 pm. My entire family was there to receive me at the doorstep, and everyone felt relieved and were happy to see me. I was about to step in when my mother asked me to drop my bag and follow her. She took me to the bedroom and locked the door. She asked me to show if I was beaten or had bruises anywhere. I saw her concern and she had tears in her eyes. She wanted to ensure my body doesn't have marks of being beaten. I assured her that I was lucky, and I wasn't hit or beaten by anyone, though a few of my good friends were hurt! She was so concerned that she even asked me to take off my shirt and show marks, if any. I had never seen her so concerned or anxious, she almost behaved as if I were in a war, truly I was, just not by my choice!

Once she was sure that I was fine & not hurt, she hugged me and blessed me, she was extremely at ease. She wiped her tears and said something that is stuck in my head even today, this one statement makes my stance easy in all life and death situation, she said, "Remember one thing, I didn't carry you nine months in my womb so that any random guy on the street comes and slaps you, you can be ordinary, but my son - he is not! Don't ever come home exploited or being dominated by anyone when you aren't wrong! If you are at fault, apologize, face the consequence but when you are not and you come home like a coward, I would disown you as my child!"

To this moment, I have never forgotten this talk from my mother. It is easier to face anything and anyone the moment I think that it's about her and not me. She raised me not to be ordinary. Be it treating women, fighting battles or loving people, she always taught the right vs. wrong lessons, yet this one talk took all the fear off me. After all, you can be weak and ordinary, yet do you really think your mother's daughter or son can be? Ask yourself - everything in the world gets easier and fear takes a back seat!

I went back to college and more troubles welcomed me, but I was able to face it. There were times when I felt Shyam would kill me to death and I faced it diplomatically, sometimes bent and begged, sometimes faced fearlessly. I was evolving, I knew I was going to come back to him stronger someday and time would come, but only if I am alive and sustained. If something had happened to me in the battleground of life in college, my mother would have never forgiven herself for the pep talk – this motivated me to ensure that I also come out safe and strong and not let her regret instilling fearlessness in me. Hence I knew what was needed, not forgiveness, but patience until the time is right!

We are in 2024 and several times in life I feel like giving up, yet, you know what?

"I can give up but my mother's son, he can't, he shouldn't, he won't!"

By now, you should know – this is for every mother raising her child with both pain and wisdom. Every time you submit to a situation, a failure, a circumstance, you are belittling a woman's pride who raised you.

This chapter is of profound significance, above all chapters, especially in today's world where sexual assault, domestic violence, abuse, crime, murders, and all sorts of inhuman acts still persist.

Life forces us to make a choice – whether to run away like a deer or hunt like a lion. Yet in the human world, we must learn to be both. Darwin's theory needs a new version - survival of the wisest! Be wise to run or hunt, yet in a longer run, build eye contact with the world, either at work or at home!

An important aspect, 'I gave up initially over Shyam's atrocities and dominance, survived the situation and after a year came back stronger when he wasn't prepared, yet in the equation of life, I averaged out with him!' The only way you would ever gather the strength to come back stronger when someone troubled you, is when you know your intent is right, else apologize and move if you wronged someone, just like my mother said, APOLOGIZE!

Intent is power, it is perseverance; intent is the differentiator between a murderer and a solider! Intent

can be a discriminator in every situation. Intent is the next chapter of this book. Adil especially testified that the value of INTENT is the most essential thing he ever learnt from our conversations and that changed his perspective towards career, life, family and self.

∞

By now you should know - this is for every mother raising her child with both pain and wisdom. Everytime you submit to a situation, a failure, a circumstance, you are belittling a woman's pride who raised you.

CHAPTER 9

INTENT

Intent is not just a tenet or philosophy; it is a fact that can be categorized to determine the outcome.

More often than not, this term is among the most difficult to truly comprehend. Attributes like nervousness, being impulsive, bad listening, being judgmental – most of these shall be resolved if an individual works thoroughly to identify the intent behind his or her actions.

March, 2024,
Boisar, Mumbai:

My father was one among seven siblings. Four brothers and three sisters. He was the third child. My uncle, Rajeshwar Mishra, 57 years old, passed away due to a stroke on his way back from work. I received a call at 11.30 am from my father and I flew from Bangalore to Mumbai in the next few hours. The subsequent morning, we planned to cremate him in the nearest possible crematorium.

Boisar in the district of Palghar is a relatively popular town near Mumbai, towards the Gujarat border, owing to several odd and good reasons. Let me tell you the reasons - Shardul Thakur, a popular figure in Indian International cricket, studied at my school in Boisar; the brutal killing of two Sadhus by a misled mob also happened in Palghar the same district as mine, it was captured on camera and also made it to the news a few years ago.

My Uncle's house was in the Gram Panchayat of Village Pasthal. Cremation procedure, death certificate, wood arrangement, everything is an operational challenge in these areas if you do not have good contacts. When I reached there, I knew and reaffirmed that I had to play a significant role in handling the family situation there. My aunt and her three kids were devastated and clueless about the next steps. Cousins were helping, yet the savior for us was Hrithik.

I didn't use the name Hrithik to confuse or grab attention. Sagar Panicker was born in 1999 and was my good friend's brother. The year 2000 was the year when Hrithik Roshan starrer, Kaho Na Pyaar Hai became a mega hit. For the next 3 years, every young boy wanted to be addressed as Hrithik. Sagar was 2–3 years old when I used to cuddle and play with him. He would keep calling himself Hrithik, and so did we. I had deep affection for him since then and he was my favorite. I myself was merely 13 years old then.

Sagar came there and said, "Shiv bhaiya, I am there, I'll handle everything."

I asked him, "Sagar, how do you know me? Did we meet before?"

He responded, "Bhaiya, Bhul gaye kya? Mein Hrithik, Hrithik Panicker, apka favourite!" ("Bhaiya, you forgot me? I am Hrithik, Hrithik Panicker, your favorite.") I couldn't believe, the small kid, was a 24-year-old handsome boy. He was built strong, firm posture and looked disciplined.

He had a workforce of young boys who followed his instructions; I saw an empathetic leader in the making. From there on, he took control of arranging everything.

The next morning around 11 am, we reached for the funeral. Hrithik, my cousins and I, lifted the body and walked for 2.5 kms to reach the cremation center. It was a tough moment, we had to video call the entire family to show the last rituals. My father's generation was old by now, and for them to travel in this time pressure wasn't easy; moreover, since everything happened suddenly, they were shocked and emotionally broken. They needed to accept the cruel fact of life that took their youngest away.

We did the 'Agni arpan' (The Hindu ritual of burning the body) and most of my school friends visited me there to meet and share their condolences. We were almost in acceptance of the change and I kind of settled there, talking to my school friends, when Hrithik called my name, "Shiv bhaiya, come here!"

The cremation center was beside a bridge over 'Vanganga river'. Hrithik came to me and said, "Shiv bhaiya, I'll show you something. Come, this would be an experience!" He took me to the river edge, where in a broken pipe, a snake was stuck. I could see the snake's tail moving. It was grayish and thick. I couldn't judge the length yet it looked massive. Hrithik softly pulled the giant snake out. He was very gentle yet firm, and in a few seconds, he began walking upwards towards the bridge. I went closer and asked him if I could record. I began recording, I asked him how he got to know that the snake doesn't have venom?

"Bhaiya, this snake can bite, it has venom, most likely one won't survive long if it bites!" I was a few inches away from the snake while recording, I was shocked, however, I didn't step back. Somehow the way he was holding, it didn't feel harmful at all. I kept walking as he left the snake back in the trees, a few meters away. The snake moved and vanished in a while.

I was confused, I had never seen such a gesture or experienced this ever. I wanted to know more. "Hrithik, how did you know that the snake won't bite you?"

He answered, "Bhaiya, a snake can sense your intent faster than a human! Just by touch."

"What do you mean by intent?" I further enquired.

"Bhaiya, with your touch, they know if it is to harm them or to care for them! It is just the way lie detector machines can see through you, intent is a critical aspect of every human behavior!"

I couldn't believe that someone could conquer a giant reptile, just by intent.

I further asked, "How many snakes have you tackled like this? Is this a proven method?"

"I have handled over 200 snakes, Bhaiya, I don't remember the count yet, I have been bitten thrice!" He responded.

He showed his right hand, which had a miserable mark like a surgical cut and looked brutal for most of the area.

"This is insane, you could have died!" I exclaimed.

"Bhaiya, it wasn't the snake's fault. For the first two times, I was learning the art, and the third time, I tried showing off! I was lifting the snake to show the crowd that I can handle them! I presume the snake judged me and hence this mark. I have undergone massive surgery to get rid of that snake's venom. It was a life and death situation, but I sailed through!" He replied calmly.

"You didn't try to kill the snake, so why would it bite you then?" I probed further.

"I don't have the right to endorse a snake to people that I don't own, the snake, after a point, knew I was not trying to save it, but rather to show off!" He responded.

"How can this be bad intent? How can you still handle snakes after that experience?" I couldn't wrap my head around it and asked.

"Intent was definitely not right; I would have never known if the snake had not bitten me! Thanks to the snake, now I never rescue anyone for show off, I do it because it's to save a life! I do it since I love animals, they don't have emotions or intelligence as per our definition, and this brings them closer to a life threat, because of us! I showed you in an attempt to bring more and more participation for such a noble cause. The pipe in the river wasn't made by animals, we manhandle nature and do this to them!"

Hrithik taught me an important lesson for life, 'INTENT'!

Sept. 2009,
Alandi, Pune:

Dr. K. P. Fernandes was my college Principal - an IIT alumnus, and a popular figure amongst the university students. He used to design the Mechanics Paper for first-year students - comprising Statics and Dynamics. Majorly inspired by Beer and Johnson's reference book on Mechanics, Dr. K. P. Fernandes used to set all questions as numerical, with an average pass rate of 13% in our university. Anyone from Pune University can validate the fact that he was 24 x 7 under the influence of alcohol and was a chain smoker. Everyone including trustees knew about his alcohol consumption issue, however, what stood out was his extreme value system at work and personal life. He would mostly join all the Quiz events - be it mythology, science, history or Geography, any question passed on to the audience would be finally passed to him if unanswered, since he would always know the answer. In my four years of student life, no quiz ever had a question that was not correctly answered by him.

I can again write an entire biography of Dr. K. P. Fernandes and his preachings, my entire value system is majorly influenced by the learning's from Dr. K. P. Fernandes.

We had an engineer's day celebration, and he was supposed to give his closing speech after the event. I would usually sit in the front row for his speech, owing to two reasons, we all loved listening to him and secondly, he knew I would remember all his speeches and content. I was one of his favorites, he liked assertive people.

"I asked Shiv not to arrange my speech at the end, nobody likes Karela after Gulab Jamun!"(nobody likes bitter gourd after eating a sweet dessert)

Everyone laughed, and he continued.

"I want to ask a simple thing to all of you guys, what's more important, to be an engineer or a human or both?"

"Two weeks ago, I was at the Nasik Phata when an accident took place, a man almost lost his one leg as he fell off his bike and came underneath a car; I asked the driver to stop the vehicle and rushed to help the man! In a few minutes, as we were trying to get the guy into ambulance, suddenly our college staff bus driver approached me."

"Sir, kuch help chahiye? Aap theek ho?" He enquired if I wanted any help.

Sir continued in rage, "He got down from the bus, parked it aside and came over to ask if help was needed – to a perfectly abled man - simply because that man is the director of his institution. Meanwhile, all these asses, your teachers, sitting in the front row were looking off the window. They bloody didn't care to get down and help the victim, not that the help we did wasn't enough, while the driver is more worried about a pseudo-designated college Director! This is the value system we carry, we lack basic human values, the intent to be a human first before being a great Engineer. Engineers are bloody problem solvers to make the world a better place, if you can't connect to humans, you will fail to cater to the ecosystem of the world, universe! I don't want such graduates from my college, build your value system, your intent should be to help someone you can, and your degree shall follow!"

Period.

Intent is quite a difficult chapter; it is difficult to internalize this term since it mostly has layers to decipher before you know yours. However, to make it easier to decipher Intent, I am moving on to the next chapter, 'The Art of Not Taking Things Personal.'

∞

DIGITAL
EVIDENCE

CHAPTER 10

THE ART OF NOT TAKING THINGS PERSONAL

Aug. 2016, Bangalore:

We had German delegates in our office, it was my first company, and we were heading for a corporate dinner. Near the lift, we engaged in small talk. The German colleagues and I had an exchange on the expenses of Indian weddings vs. German weddings. It is a known fact that Indian weddings are much more expensive than a German wedding. The costliest thing in a German wedding is the bride's gown, while in an Indian wedding, that's barely 10 percent of the overall expense. We were criticizing the unwanted expense on Indian weddings when my department head Vidit, pitched in, he said, "We spend so much because mostly we get married only once! Hahaha!"

The satire didn't land well, we all paused, the Germans saw finger pointing on the ratio of divorces in Germany vs. India. I personally couldn't believe that my department head mocked our delegates. We paused for a minute and continued.

After a couple of days, I was driving with my ex-boss and mentor Vinay Kamath, who is still my godfather in the Automotive Electronics Industry, we were like friends more than him being my boss. I shared this instance with him and judged my department head for being lame and sarcastic to our guests. I mentioned that I expected more maturity from him, otherwise, Vidit was a fine leader and an extremely assertive professional at work. I was a quarter of his experience, yet he always offered me space to be myself and promoted a speak-up culture. I somehow never wanted to judge Vidit this way, yet I knew this time I did!

Vinay gave me a perspective that hit me hard, "Shiv, high chances that Vidit didn't even think of them, he was just talking about himself! Weren't we together at his spouse's funeral three years ago? He has two kids and for them, he decided to never get married again!"

I was ashamed of myself; I remember when Vidit rushed from the office at 3 pm, hearing the news of his wife's unexpected demise due to an asthma attack while taking a shower. The kids were sleeping upstairs in his duplex and could not hear their mother asking for help. The entire night we were all with Vidit, he was crying like a kid, creating several narratives of how if he had not been at work that day, he could have saved his wife. He had an 8-year-old son and a 12-year-old daughter then. He decided to never get married again and took care of his kids as his only life goal. He didn't think about anyone other than his case when he said that simple and profound thing. While German colleagues and I took the conversation as sarcasm that didn't land well, we equally took the comment personal; on the contrary, he too took the wedding conversation personal, associated himself more with it. Can we really detach ourselves from an objective conversation? If we can, we certainly fall in the category, "I don't take things personal!"

A recent rape episode in Kolkata shook the entire world. It happened in a medical college. Most of my friends on insta accused men of being bad, worst, and inhuman. They went on making memes about how the world of men is unsafe. I felt insecure and uncomfortable reading posts in every other story.

"Shrivarshiny, the rapist men are not on the insta handle in your friend-list, why are all women sharing such posts to us? We are not rapists or women offenders! I feel so bad for the girl who was victimized, yet I am afraid we are targeting the wrong crowd! We also have sisters, and it is so hurtful as we equally feel concerned about them and wish to kill the evil in the society for once and for all, why target us?"

"Shiv, when someone dies, their family goes and posts on social media in their remembrance a few days after they accept the loss, there are times people also write on the wall of the person dead and share their mind!" explained Shri.

She continued, "Does it mean that they are in the digital world talking to the ghost of the dead? They are just venting out; they are simply sharing their pain and grief. This time is to sympathize with them and understand that they aren't questioning you; instead, when you respond by commenting, they feel they are a team. When we say the world of humans is so bad, do we really include us, the ones in conversation? We in totality address the ill and evil human, it is obvious."

I always found her perspectives clear, crisp, and way ahead of her age. She helped me understand a basic fact once again: I was taking something personal.

I then shared the same posts from my female friends in my story and lots of men and women reacted in support. I felt like I was a part of a digital revolution. It felt much better and easy to understand what the intent of the post was. I wish I could master the art of, not taking things personal. You may criticize the book if you genuinely don't find it helpful, my reaction might be a better testimony to this aspect.

∞

Not taking things personal, is an internal factor, it's a mindset, while its application or front-end use case is demonstrated easily by the way we receive feedback. There are many layers to this art of taking feedback.

I can bet on the fact that the next chapter is way easier to understand and the most difficult to practice. I mastered this art a few years ago. I'll try to simplify.

CHAPTER 11

FEEDBACK: LISTENING

March 2023,
Kolkata:

We were on IIM C campus attending the last guest lecture by ex-Chairman IRCTC, Ex Managing Director, Air India, and Limca book of world records holder, Mr. Ashwani Lohani. He shared his stories during his time serving railways, aviation as well as Madhya Pradesh tourism department.

Extraordinary energy, to the point conversation and interesting anecdotes from his leadership times.

"Shiv, why don't you ask your question from yesterday to Mr. Lohani!" Suggested Vikrant.

Vikrant, Vivek, Harsh and Tamagna - we were best buddies from the batch and termed as backbenchers. We were notorious yet curious students of our batch, with an average 17+ years of industrial experience, we barely behaved our age, we remained the child not caring about career, yet we stayed inquisitive about the context.

I raised my hand the moment the forum opened for Q and A. I eventually struggled, yet someone passed on the mic to me in the order of being the fourth one asking the question. People, by now, were tired yet attentive.

"Sir, I feel too small in front of you asking this question, yet allow me to ask one!" The moment I said this, I sensed the energy of the crowd drop low. There was a sense of disappointment for some reason, I couldn't explain to myself why, yet my intuitive self sensed it.

"Sir, most organizations have multiple departments, and all the heads of their domains tend to be capable leaders; however, every time the CEO needs a successor to herself or himself, one or two names amongst the list of contenders tend to take dominance. There is always a vibe or intuition about who could hold the throne! How are companies able to decide on identifying one amongst several successful top-notch leaders? What parameters help in such scenarios?"

I barely remember the answer; perhaps I didn't sync the question appropriately, yet the feeling of dropped energy remained in my head.

Three months later, we were preparing for our convocation ceremony - Shamit, Vishal and I were on a call planning the after-event party. We were the Organizers. Shamit dropped out and Vishal and I exchanged some informal conversations. In a few minutes, I happened to ask Vishal if he had any feedback for me. It used to be my usual practice to seek feedback from people and try to incorporate the relevant ones.

"Shiv, I don't think there is anything specific that needs improvement, you are already best in class in most of your things, yet there is one point I observed and would like to bring to your attention! Why should I listen to you if you aren't confident about your question!" Vishal asked.

"Vishal, are you referring to the question I asked Mr. Lohani?" I enquired.

"Maybe, I don't remember, but I have observed you adding too many conditional statements to your questions, perhaps not in your domain of work, because you might be more confident about what you are talking about, however, please extrapolate similar practices even in newer areas you enter! If you aren't sure, don't ask, and if you are, then don't add disclaimers showcasing yourself down!"

"You have to consciously work upon it at a few instances, and in a few months, it might become natural to you!" He further added.

I took two days to understand his feedback and correlate situations where it was applicable. It struck me that Shankar, my super-boss and one of the established leaders in the Automated Driving World, had given me similar feedback about my operating style in certain meetings. I would add some redundant disclaimers or proactive perception management lines like, "Please don't misunderstand..., I might be wrong, still hear me out...., you know better, but can I still make a point....." and so on. Going back in time, I recollected similar feedback from Vidyasagar almost ten years ago, who was our project lead in my first company, and he told me something similar. I realized how little self-aware I was despite multiple hints. Wisdom is never too late, who knew I would have to someday be live on TV and ask a simple question to a global leader like Dr. Tharoor, and that day I would not underutilize such a huge platform by doing over perception management. It is so difficult to assimilate feedback, it takes ages to build the quality to understand that the one giving feedback is your friend and not your rival!

I always believe things happen for a reason, mostly failures in this case. The encounter while asking a question to Mr. Lohani and an almost failed attempt helped me learn and seek feedback that I could implement during Dr. Tharoor's conversation. It was important to keep the question optimal and intact, I would never have done that if not for the feedback from Vishal. I have thanked him several times emphasizing the impact his feedback made on me. It has changed my operating style at work as well, made me concise, firm, and clearer.

Layers of feedback reciprocation:

I always thought I was very good at taking feedback, I always embraced the opinion and tried to act upon it; however, I felt I was not perfect at taking feedbacks, there are some layers to this process, and I haven't reached the bottom yet. Thanks to Pavan Chaithanya, a mentor for one of our Leadership Training Programs at my current organization. We were in a coffee conversation when the concept of feedback and listening surfaced. He quoted a profound statement, which hit me hard, it sums up the deepest layer of the feedback-taking mechanism.

"Even if the feedback doesn't apply to you, it is essential to respond/revert/reply only if your response has any value addition to the owner of the conversation, the one who gave you the feedback! As simple as it appears, I am still trying to master this aspect of listening."

Example:

Nayana: "Shiv, when you get married, don't be a stereotypical orthodox misogynist!"

Shiv: "Yes, Nayana, I'll ensure this" vs. "Come on Nayana, why the hell would you think this way? I am a born gentleman, raised well by my family.........." and many more to the literature or wordplay!

You see the point? If the last line isn't easy to comprehend or relate to, please go back to the chapter, "Art of not taking things personal!"

I'll move on to an independent chapter, it has no direct correlation to the previous chapter; however, it has a huge impact in building character, it has been the slowest poison that kills all segments of people.

Peer Pressure!

∞

CHAPTER 12

CONFORMITY BIAS/PEER PRESSURE

The act of getting disturbed with someone's growth, someone achieving something before you and a feeling of losing while you have lost nothing - peer pressure is a peculiar human trait coming from our chimp instincts.

It shall be easier to overcome this basic human impulse if I state a simple fact: peer pressure comes from scarcity - either of money, resources, power, or wisdom. Humans began their civilization in the times when mining resources were dependent on external factors like weather. In a community, getting your right share of food was a cold battle and at times a burning one. The same community acted as a shield to safeguard one's security and safety. The safety aspect drove the community living in us, while the limited resources like food and shelter also led us to compete. Even in recent times of corona, the whole world united to fight this difficult battle, no one wanted to get out of their doors and Prime Ministers of developed countries were seen crying. Today, as the world resumes normalcy after the massacre of corona, now wars are back to where they were. Just like how animals fight within a community while protecting each other from an external threat.

Peer pressure is unfortunate genetics, echoing this very basic human nature. In the current world, neither the weather nor the count of resources is as low as unlike then;

however, we still are unable to overcome the primitive notion within us!

Instance 1: In 2010, we had an aptitude exam for a Software tech firm. There was a question, "A house has all four walls facing towards South, a bear is making rounds around the house, which color is the bear?"

1. Pink
2. Brown
3. White
4. Black

We finished the test, and I began discussing the question. I am the same guy who comes out of exams, discusses questions, and gives a difficult time to his friends before the actual results. I usually love predicting my score.

"Bear is always black, big deal! Black it is!" replied Sonali. Sonali, in terms of her grasping, IQ and analytical skills, was way ahead of many of us. Five other friends around us nodded.

I couldn't believe how stupid I was, everyone knew the answer and I alone made the blunder. I knew I won't be getting selected since I answered the bear to be white.

By the same evening, we received information that the Placement cell made a mistake and Electronics domain students are no longer to be shortlisted further, the firm confirmed that only Computer Science and IT students are eligible. We all got rejected, yet I was still disturbed about my wrong answer.

I wondered why I focused more on the house and not on the bear, why was I so lame?

I checked into a cybercafé and verified the answer, I realized I was the only guy who got the logic right. It was an eye opener for me, I understood a simple thing, masses think alike and mostly they focus on what they find easier to do, only a minority reach the actual answer.

We were at Kirti Doongursee College in Mumbai, back in 2006, to give the IIT entrance test. I was surprised when cohorts were discussing answers with each other and trying to get their best scores during the exam. Knowing the statistics of shortlisting at IITs, the high probability was that the entire classroom might not have any shortlisting, yet many thought, "my neighbor is smarter than I am," and would know how to crack the test.

Now in 2024, I get the same feeling when many youngsters reach out to me mentioning their application for Harvard, Oxford, Durham, Sussex and many such foreign universities. By far, while I would have spoken with more than 150 plus applicants over coffee while mentoring, there was only one guy, Anshuman, an applicant for a master in Tech, who could explain why he finds the few universities as his go-to place. He stitched it to the professors there who made a difference in the technological world, he stitched to the High-tech companies that look for candidates from these universities and could also explain to me the connection between his current profile and the university thesis topics.

While the majority of others answered, "These universities are the best!"

When asked - how do you know? There won't be more content to it. Let me share an anecdote to make it simpler.

I started my career in a Multinational Automotive firm in Bangalore, back in 2010. We had Graduate Engineer Trainees' lunch with the CFO and CEO during our induction round. The CFO was a French guy, I would avoid mentioning his credentials beyond that.

He asked, "How many of you wish to go abroad for work from our firm?"

Puneet Sehgal raised his hand and none of us showed much inclination. Most of us were hesitant, while people like me, Sharath Kotian and a few others amongst us were least influenced by peer pressure. We knew if work takes us, we shall go, yet the idea of joining the firm is to deliver technology and understand business nuances.

"Which country do you want to go?" the CFO enquired.

Puneet answered, "Europe, I love European lifestyle?"

"Have you been there before?" CFO asked.

"No, I haven't!" Responded Puneet.

"Then how do you know about the European lifestyle?" The CFO contradicted.

There was a pin drop silence for a moment, facepalm for Puneet, yet, today in 2024, Puneet is leading his life in

Dusseldorf, Germany. I recently met him during my visit, and we had a great time. He quit the firm after 3 years, pursued his Masters in Germany and made his way. He is married to a German and is nicely settled.

Sharath Kotian, on the contrary, is leading as a Research and Development Head for a development department in the same firm; he is probably the youngest R&D head the firm would have ever had. I am doing fine too, in the long run, all three in the story made good with their life, what matters is if you know genuinely what you believe in or it's just a neural wiring.

The majority of people around you won't reach the destination they wish to - it is a pyramid in professional life. In personal life too, peer pressure just raises your stress levels for less or no logical reason. Evidently, at airports, you see a few entry gates overcrowded while some gates simply idle for oblivious reasons.

Biases of several kinds are interrelated, and another chapter dives deeper into it.

∞

CHAPTER 13

BREAKING THE NEURAL WIRING

We all have goals that seem farfetched or sometimes undoable or unachievable ones. Most of us often wish to be somewhere special, yet we struggle to know how and what needs to be done to get there.

There are two ways to manifest,

- Control and mend the outside world.
- Control and mend the world inside you.

The world inside you has billions of neurons, this world is your mind! It took me 3 decades to understand a simple fact: most of us visit pilgrims and holy places just to unlock this one corner of our mind, which is the corner that restores faith, trust, belief, and sometimes wisdom!

Manifestation is not that complex; it is a process of bringing yourself to the capability to attain something. Once done, the world finds you and obtains what it wants from you! If you develop the right skill and break the relevant wrong neural wiring, you can achieve mostly what you aimed for! The idea is to break neural wiring, why? Because neural wiring hampers your manifestation process. If you stick to what your brain's default is wired for, owing to its junk exposure, you lose out on rewiring the neurons when something logical and solution-based comes your way. The training of breaking neural wiring helps you bring in your outlook with rationales and not on some half-baked prejudices crafted by biased world around us.

Example:

The simplest example of neural wiring in today's Gen Z world is, Harvard and Oxford are the best universities in the world; if you ask yourself why, the answer would be: Since everyone believes so!

How to identify neural wiring,

- A context, topic, thought process or perspective proposed by someone, which your mind denies **before a conscious analysis,** is the best example of strong neural wiring.
- A context, topic, thought process or perspective that your mind denies **without building a rationale.** In fact, even if the conversationalist gives a rational argument, you tend to nod against it with a firm belief.
- If you **conclude before listening** to the whole thing, if the answer is in your head before the communicator finishes his/her narrative, it's an indicator of strong neural wiring.

Important note:

You don't have to break all the neural wirings, recognizing them is important.

∞

The world inside you has a billions of neurons, this world is your mind.

CHAPTER 14

I DO NOT MATTER: THE CONTENT DOES!

August 2009:

It was Raksha Bandhan, and my sister used to live in Pune, working for Accenture.

I was still studying - pursuing my final year. It was a college fest named "Wizard - 2010". There were several events ongoing, Business Plan being one of the key highlights. Kshitij Malhotra came to me and asked for help.

"Shiv, I don't have an audience for my event, including the judges, I am left with just 20-30 odd people in the room, I need your help!"

I immediately rushed to the lobby and announced loud and clear - "Anyone standing in the lobby doing nothing, must assemble in the conference room in 5 minutes for the business plan event, I am counting 1-10. I began counting, I was influential and assertive, the conviction in my statement didn't give them another chance to think differently. Most of them began walking towards the conference room. Few notorious ones like me, in person requested to be bailed out, I softly agreed. By now, the room was decently full, very limited chairs were left vacant.

The event was 5 minutes away. I enquired, "Kshitij, what is this business plan event? I have heard often yet never participated!"

"You have to propose a business idea, Shiv, it should have a profitable model that can earn revenue!" shared Kshitij.

"Sir, give me some examples!" I requested.

"I have less time, wait!" he further continued, "There is a business idea I saw in the previous event, of a hydroelectric power plant. The setup cost was 40 crores, and it could supply electricity to an industrial belt, making a net profit of around 3 crores a year, reducing debt!"

I responded, "This is sufficient, thanks a lot. Do I also have to sell something in real or do something other than presenting my concept? Any real exercise involved - of selling or buying?"

"No, there is none!" replied Kshitij.

"Thanks, Kshitij, you rush now, I'm good!" I asserted.

The event began and I went to the counter where a junior was giving a receipt for entry to the event. These fests would have a minimal entry fee, which eventually becomes the prize money for the winner. The entry fee was 100 bucks and as a typical backbencher, I didn't have any money. I asked the student to give the receipt with a note behind that the payment is due. I told him that I'll pay this money once I'm done with the contest. The idea was to pay him by lending it from another friend; however due to less time left in hand, I decided to do that after the event is done.

Group 1: Had a dairy processing plant proposal. The investment was around 1.5 crores and half of it was debt while the remaining was investment. They were the winners of the university event and were reiterating a winning script and concept. They faced a few questions from judges on competitor strategy.

The moment I heard these guys, I began drafting my slides, which were purely for my reference. I decided to use the whiteboard for the modelling and explanation of my business concept. I decided to scribble on the whiteboard. I asked people around me to ensure they raise their hand when I ask a question, "Who amongst you all likes playing Snooker?" Sonali also nodded, "Shiv, I'll raise my hand too!" I gave her a look and told her to join me on the stage, I need a partner, else they would presume I am not a team player. She said, "You yourself don't know what the business plan is and there are just 4 more teams to go before us!"

I told her - "No, we are going next, right after them!" I mentioned this and she almost jumped off the chair. I waved at Kshitij and asked him to call me next, when group 1 was almost done presenting. Kshitij reasoned with me through his expressions, twice, and asked me to take some time and prepare well. I insisted and right then, Kshitij called me out on the stage. Dipti Sakhre ma'am, who is now the HoD of the Electronics Department of MIT, Alandi college, was one of the judges alongside two professors from the MBA division. I took the marker and went close to the whiteboard.

"I am sorry everyone, we are beginners in our entrepreneurial journey and hence do not have enough investment to rent out a laptop. In the interest of ROI, we would use a whiteboard that comes free of cost. Our business concept is a Snooker club services company. Let me ask the crowd, "How many of you play snooker here? See, almost 25 people in a room of 100, love playing Snooker." If I consider a population of 2000 people in a college, I clearly see a target market of 500 people who might be my potential customers. Assuming my calculation can go wrong, I would consider my target market to be just 50 people, which is 10% of the estimated target crowd.

A snooker club is nonproductive from 9 to 12 noon in the majority of clubs. I proposed a snooker business with a net profit of INR 24K per month, excluding rental expenses for utilizing the space of an existing club owner, who would mostly not see any footfall until 11-12 noon. I also suggested that the price of the table per hour could be easily negotiated in the non-productive hours of the business. An overall investment of 500 INR to print 500 copies of snooker tournament papers and bike fuel expenses as additional. With an entry fee of 60 INR in the days when a Snooker table would cost 60-70 INR per hour and on unproductive hours could be 60% of the price, the concept was a clear-cut 24K INR net profit model.

Futurist view: Expand the business in a span of 2 years across 25 such college areas without any asset investment.

Long-term growth: Cover 5 top cities of India in a span of 10 years, organically.

Whiteboard crux:

> 50 Entries: 60 INR each, overall entry fee: 3000 INR
>
> Prize money to the winner: 700 INR to the winner.
>
> Overall table rental deduction:
>
> (40 INR per hour table rental cost, approximately two-three matches in one hour. Number of matches needed for 50 entries, 25 knock outs + 13 qualifiers + 6 quarter finals + 3 + 2+1)
>
> Number of matches: 50: Needs 21 hours. Each hour cost: 40 INR, overall cost: 840 INR
>
> Net profit: ~1500 INR. Each day.
>
> ***~ 8 Saturdays and Sundays in a month and two weekdays evening hours accounted, there could be four tournaments per week, 16 per month: Overall net profit from one college area: 24000 INR.***
>
> Based on the number of colleges, the business could expand and additional one referee cost deduction at each venue, the compounding might happen over the course of time.

I finished my presentation and there was pin drop silence. Nobody had ever seen a lame proposal of earning 24K INR in a business plan contest. Moreover, the project in ten years was to earn what my dairy industry friend would earn in a year with risks involved, while in my business plan there is no asset and no liability.

"I shall buy a laptop costing 40K once my business runs for 2 years, perhaps I won't use the whiteboard after that!" There were claps after this. Judges didn't ask any questions; they didn't know if there was any flaw in the proposal. The scale of the business was too low to have complexity.

Someone from the audience asked, "60 INR is too high, customers won't turn up!"

"How much do you think customers would find OK to pay as entry?" I enquired.

"I don't know, maybe 40 INR?"

"Alright, makes sense. I will reduce my profit to be just 15K per month and reduce the entry fee to 40 INR." I responded.

I know it sounds heroic, like a movie show, however, with fond memories and a certificate of the contest attached below in the chapter, we won the event - securing the first position. Kshitij came to me and asked, "Buddy, you knew how the business plan event works? You already had a proposal, and you fooled us?"

Little did he know, the only good thing that happened to me was, I didn't know how business plan contests run. If I knew it, I would have followed the masses and most likely presented a pseudo-business model that I would never pursue in real life. I won 600 INR prize money, of which I returned 100 bucks to the junior who trusted me with the receipt, I didn't fail to live up to my commitment too.

I visited the city that evening and gave the remaining

money to my sister, Santoshi Mishra Pathak, as the prize money. She still has the money preserved as she found this special. In 2021, October, I set up my father's snooker club in BTM layout, Bangalore, named - 'It's a Snook'. All the videos on my Insta handle playing snooker are from my club. Owing to Papa's retirement and age, we ended up selling the business in 2024 to a friend who was equally passionate.

I have failed in a few elocution and debate contests. There have been times when I fumbled on stage, in 8th class, when I ended up making fun of myself in front of a bigger audience. Everyone laughed, this was when I was already popular as a speaker. It happened once again in class 11 when I spoke about Fashion, which I couldn't relate to.

Building content comes with observations, simple thinking and rational building. Observations are the primary preparation for building content in your speech. I couldn't speak or ideate, articulate, and execute well in any situation unless I related to the topic in totality and reality. True content, business ideas, creative art come based on your observations and learning while you aren't preparing for them. I spent 6-7 hours every day during college time in the snooker club and the idea of picking something I genuinely know vs. what I might hypothetically imagine is the difference between fluid and simple content vs complex content, which might be spiral to your own success story. Content is what you live in the lazy hours of your life, content is the movies you watch, the people you see while travelling, the concepts you learn while you don't have an agenda behind, content in a nutshell are things that fall in front of your eyes without a deliberate intent of seeing it.

'What plays a significant role in the process of endorsing content without hesitation? To rehearse and affirm yourself, "I DO NOT MATTER, the content does!" Every time you think you are someone important and special, you create performance pressure and perhaps confuse between most relevant content vs. what might sound most relevant. This takes the right content away from the listener. I was inspired by the narrative in Mahatma Gandhi's book 'My Experiments with Truth'. The author mentions how truth prevails when you consider yourself and your ego lighter than dust. Once you walk on the stage considering yourself to be nothing, every conversation becomes easier than you ever thought it would.

∞

DIGITAL
EVIDENCE

CHAPTER 15

THE CONVINCING LIE: CONVERGENCE OF ALL CHAPTERS

July 2012 marked the beginning of salary corrections for 2010 batch graduate engineer trainees, who had just been confirmed following the successful completion of their probation. I was one of those, who wasn't offered the correction, in fact, I was the only one on that list. After my first boss, Mr. Anubhav Sharma, stepped down from his role as a Senior Manager and eventually left the firm, my performance rating declined from 'Excellent' to 'Meets expectations' over the course of a year and a half. Anubhav Sir, who had also interviewed me, was well acquainted with my working style and often referred to me as an all-rounder. My new boss, Suresh Sir, on the other hand, was a former ISRO Class 1 officer. He was someone who had struggled a lot yet always sailed through owing to his discipline and commitment, exactly the things I wasn't wired to adhere to.

I had an attitude problem too. For instance, when my team leader would ask me to compare two micro-controller schematic designs, I would ask her more about why I should compare it? What would she do with the comparison report? I was expected to see how many capacitors, resistors and diodes remained common across the boards and list those which were unique to each of them. She would come back by evening, and I would most likely not have completed the work.

I was also quite fearless. I would do continuous chatting on the phone and browse Facebook on our office computer. This was pissing everyone off, for obvious reasons. When asked why I am not doing the task, I would say I am not able to focus since I was not able to comprehend the bigger picture. I was also one of the first trainees in the team, hence, they had no idea how to groom me. I used to fill excise sheets, do SAP data entry, solder PCB boards and wait for that one project which would give me a kick, however, I always enjoyed the clerical jobs. It was a top-notch firm, however, the team was just established, hence work of all sorts was offered. This pattern continued until one day I was called into a meeting room by the General Manager and my own boss.

"Shiv, we haven't given you any correction, you are the only one in the batch whom we decided not to offer any salary upgrade, moreover, we also feel you aren't fit for the firm. You aren't doing your job, and you are always chatting on the phone." This was unexpected, I didn't know that perceptions had gone so bad. I was merely 22 years old; I needed someone to hold me and take me out of the situation, perhaps predict what would happen next!

"Does it mean, I am fired?" I was worried.

"You aren't fired, however, we would recommend you look for a job elsewhere, we shall give you time!" responded the General Manager.

"I am working on the Body Control Module project bench development; can I finish the project and go?" I was hopeful. They expected retaliation and an aggressive response, I suppose.

"How long is the project for? Is it for the Indian customer xxxx?"

"Yes, I would need 2-3 months to complete the project, then I could leave!"

"No, let us consider this as your chance to prove yourself, certainly we have an HR process to put you under probation again, and we could set this as your target!" he responded.

"I don't need any of those, I just need one favor, 2.5 months and no team leader over me! I'll do the project without Vidit and Sreeja!" It was a test bench to test the body control module for a USA carmaker's Indian project. We had a few quality issues with the product that sits inside the car and handles critical functions. The Car maker wanted us to provide proactive test bench to be stationed in their premises to test the electronic functions like power windows, wiper functions, speed parameters and several others like the auto door lock functions. This was indeed one classic project which I was certain to visualize in my head end-to-end. It was much easier than my fourth-year engineering project, the only constraint was that I didn't want to follow the traditional way my leads would suggest. Moreover, they could barely deal patiently with me, they were annoyed. They weren't at fault, they expected obedience, I perhaps didn't know what that meant!

"How would you develop an entire hardware test bench alone? You need people to support you? You don't have competence? You are a fresher almost!"

"I am unable to work with the team leaders since they expect me to behave like a fresher, exactly what I do not understand! I can handle this; maybe at the end of the exercise you might feel this was a good experience to see a positive outcome?"

"We agree, sure go ahead. Once done, we will review your work. I think it's too early to think the other way round, let us give you this chance."

I stepped out of the room and had tears. I knew I was a good chap, I knew I wasn't wrong by intent however, somehow the world couldn't see through me. Perhaps I lacked direction, however, I had a firm intent to contribute. The team leaders would judge based on what time I would come to work, they never looked into my final year project (times of India coverage of my final year project attached at the end of the chapter), the skills I carried and many other things. I had mixed feelings, yet was determined to battle this out, not like a winner but like a survivor.

Those 27 days, I came to work at 8 am instead of 10 am like I used to earlier, back in 2011-12, coming to work at 10 am was a big offence, especially in non-IT industries like ours. I finished the whole project in 27 days. I remember using IC-555 monostable multivibrator timer, it was the 4th or 5th chapter of Engineering Electronics subject in our semester 2 of graduation.

The China team had quoted 4000 Euros for a simple test bench which for me was seamlessly a third-year engineering project. Even the labels for the switches I bought from a local printing franchise called Printo. The whole project was ready in half the size and 150 Euros overall cost, which in INR was merely 11000. Consulting colleagues like Swaraj Pattoth and Vikas Singapur helped; they guided me wherever I lacked experience. I worked every day, including weekends. I decided to solder the whole bench on my own, I remember sometimes I would be so tired and stressed wondering what my life would be after 27 days. I would end up pinching the soldering gun into my hand instead of the PCB board, I still have a few minor marks. Apart from talking to Papa and sister, I had no one who would come and say, "I am here, I'll protect you!" Whenever I caught up with a few of my seniors at the breakfast table, they would scare me more by mentioning how judgements about me are indicative of my bad performance. A person of my mindset who could defeat G B Syndrome, causing paralysis just six months ago was now losing it all. I was scared, worried and eventually began calling my sister for help. I was close to a mental breakdown. She guided me to avoid anything and anyone who feels toxic, including my colleagues who affected my mental health. She said - "You need to avoid anyone who is adding to your stress!" Papa supported that idea too. I began avoiding all types of toxic people around me and focused on my delivery. I kept clocking 12-14 hours to eagerly finish my work. Honestly, none of them were wrong or evil, it was just lack of empathy, no wonder the industry spends millions of dollars to train people to be empathetic. Some of us are born with that trait before even knowing the word existed!

I narrated the story in my version where I am a victim, when I look back, I am able to see through all their perspectives, few of them were right and rational because there was a problem they wanted to solve in me, while the others needed mentors themselves.

After a month, when the test equipment was tested to be OK, the opinions moderately took a back seat and somehow basic trust was restored. My job was saved, however, I still continued to take a corner in the room, clueless. 'Clueless' is not just a word, it is an adage, a proverb in fact, sometimes the point before wisdom, only if you recognize and embrace it. Everyone in this world needs direction, you got to keep moving.

One fine day we had a visitor from Germany, Dr. Andreas Nestler, our technology head Global. He was going to retire in six months and wanted to make his last visit to align for near-future strategies. My little tester box also made its way next to all complex systems in the lab. This was categorized under freshers project contribution despite my two-year completion, one reason could be that the test bench looked too minimalistic in a world where technology is supposed to be complex, even in appearance. I got a call from Sagar, "Shiv, can you come to the lab quickly!"

As I entered, someone from the presenters' side mentioned that I had developed the equipment. "Would you please go to China and provide them with knowledge on how to develop simple, cost-effective solutions? They want to make a sun to power one house, I am sometimes frustrated with the money we are bleeding!"

Something changed, many things changed, that one moment changed the perception of an entire room. I was happy, emotional, and yet normal. When I look back it gives me goosebumps remembering those moments; however, back then I was still at status quo, the status was #clueless!

A few months passed and I was handed over my hike letter with a 25 percent upgrade over my current salary. I still remember, one of my good friends (who had very recently joined the firm with close to 8 years' experience), Vinay Kamath said, "Shiv, 15% is what you earned and 10% is the management's acceptance of misjudging your caliber! Keep it up!" My fate took good turns from this day and in four months from then, Vinay Kamath became my boss. He was offered this #clueless team of clueless people whom he turned into wonders! He still is my Godfather and someone who proudly says, "Avanu na'mma Huduga!" in Kannada that means I am his disciple, result of his grooming. I still bow down to him, he offered me to work on a full-fledged project for the Indian market, which benchmarked my automotive journey.

Shridhar San, my first coach and mentor in the industry, taught me invaluable corporate lessons over casual conversations at chai tapris, someone whom I always looked up to, for developing integrity and wisdom. As I was preparing to leave the firm in 2017, he narrated to me a flashback story, he said, "Shiv, I once asked Vinay -

what do you see in Shiv that you trust him so much, as per his previous boss and most leads, he isn't fit for the job?" This was somewhere during my struggling period. To which Vinay replied, "Shridhar, Shiv at the age of 22 has a strong perspective! Every time we talk about anything, he has strong and firm views about things, situations and circumstances! This cannot come to a person without content. Perhaps his orientation cannot be like majority of people in the industry, you've got to throw him into the ocean, he would swim, yet if you put him into a swimming pool and ask him to learn how to swim, he might not turn up the next day!"

March 2025,
Atria Institute of Technology:

I was invited by the Engineering college as a guest for their annual tech fest event. Instead of talking about AI and Deep tech changing the world, I was triggered to talk about 'imperfections'! Why? Simply because a young tech-savvy alumnus of the college, while addressing the crowd during the inauguration, fumbled on the stage. Instead of pulling himself back, he decided to accept, embrace and continue his speech. Despite things not going his way, he continued to deliver his message and ended up sharing strong content. All I did was cheer him in between when we recognized his struggle in the beginning.

I realized, no matter which era and generation we are in, the idea of being imperfect and being ok with it needed attention since no one talks about it. I themed my speech as, "My Imperfect Father!"

I shared a few anecdotes of my father's style of raising an ordinary, below-average child like me. Instead of praising me while I scored 40/40 in class 8th, he asked me, "You learnt function f(x), where would you use it in real life?" I was, as always, clueless! He further added, "If you do not know real-life use cases of things you study, you are not 40/40, sorry Son!"

It took me 3 days and a lot many thoughts to come back to Papa and share, "Papa, I can use a function f(a) to define the corner of our room to a civil engineer. I can call it, f(a) = x + y + z, and define the length, width and height of the room! If I represent all corners with a function like this, a civil engineer can document the dimensions of the entire room."

"I am happy today, you scored 100/40!" This was my father's response.

The most convincing lie that the world tells you is, your grades decide your fate. I do not mean scoring less is OK, I mean scoring high means nothing different than scoring low if you do not know where to use what you study!

By the end of my speech, I shared several anecdotes like these, blending laughter and wisdom through the stories and actions of my father. I am the most ordinary, below-average child, who was lucky to have three world-class parents in my life. Mother who gave me courage, Sister who improved my intelligence and father who taught me the art of distinguishing between truth and lie. Scoring the best doesn't make you the best; relating real life to education certainly does.

At the end of my speech, I asked, "Is there anyone in this room who feels she or he is #clueless and cannot figure out what to do next?" I iterated a couple of times when two gentlemen, young chaps, raised their hand. I said, "I would mentor you, I won't give you jobs nor give you internships, this is much more, I am signing to ensure the next ten years of your life, I am there to get the best of your days!" It has been three weeks since their training began, training which helps them discover themselves, training that helps them identify lie in every single narrative, training that helps them decide what they want from the world and not what the world offers them, training that my father gave me, the training that brings the best of the average, the training to embrace being #clueless and imperfect!

The book is not designed to tattle my readers about what is right or what is wrong, it is designed to discover the best version of you, the version that snakes can sense, the version that guides a mother her way, the version that tells why it is ok to be better than your boss, the version that respects content over people and also the version who practices empathy before knowing the word!

It is easy to break down the sequence of me appearing on the ABP show that brought a platform to put across a sincere question that, as a child, resonated in me.

Questions looming from Chapter 1 - those are answered below,

How did I get the microphone? Was it a sheer coincidence?

- I raised a firm hand.
- The decision was quick.
- Clarity of thought

How did I reach the venue, how and why was I invited?

- Playing Guitar: A skill I learnt to discover myself.
- Eagerness to enroll in a course and learn.
- Trusting the process of valuing experiences, the reason why I flew all the way to Mumbai.
- I don't know why I was invited; Parul perhaps can answer that!

How did I execute the simple conversation at a complex platform comfortably?

- Content: The question was important, but I wasn't!

The strongest factor of all was, how did I reach there?

~~It was my luck, fortune. Luck favors and people make it big!!!!! Period~~

This is the most convincing lie society feeds into your mind!

The truth, which isn't convincing nor stereotyped, however is the truest to its form,

Run towards excellence, success is a byproduct.

Even to successfully address a 2 minute question on a global platform, took me years of self-adherence and focus. Imagining what it shall take to be at the Dias on the other side, facing the crowd, it is not predictable yet what needs to be done to reach such a place is constant perseverance, strong and right intent and working on 1 billion neurons within you!

∞

Luck can be designed with strong intent and content! Let that sync in.

DIGITAL
BOOK

Shiv is an everyday ordinary person doing extraordinary things. Professionally he is an automotive enthusiast with 15 years of experience in Autonomous Driving Technology and Embedded systems. Currently, serving as a Program Manager at premiere automotive firm, holds credentials from MITAOE and IIMC.

He's a back bencher by heart and has been caught bunking multiple lectures, chasing professors over coffee rather than in class. Beyond work, he's an enthusiastic self-taught snooker player, debater, fitness enthusiast, reader, singer, investor and a lot more, a mix of energy and curiosity through everything he does. His version of solving a Rubik's cube is to not solve it as faster than usual, rather solve it slow until he discovers how the first person solving it must have felt.

Anyone who knows Shiv would describe him as an exemplary friend and an invested mentor. His empathy and care for people, community, his work and country are at the forefront of how he lives life. The book is an honest attempt to declutter the noise of mainstream media on how to live life and by extension become successful. Its aim is to help people find their most authentic self by sharing anecdotes from Shiv's own life experiences. Something that he believes is very rarely talked about in today's world.